J. T Lindsay

French Exiles of Louisiana

J. T Lindsay

French Exiles of Louisiana

ISBN/EAN: 9783743311015

Manufactured in Europe, USA, Canada, Australia, Japa

Cover: Foto ©Thomas Meinert / pixelio.de

Manufactured and distributed by brebook publishing software
(www.brebook.com)

J. T Lindsay

French Exiles of Louisiana

LEAVING HOME.

"He turned and gazed upon the dear scenes of his childhood."　Page 26.

FRENCH EXILES

OF

LOUISIANA.

BY

J. T. LINDSAY,

AUTHOR OF "LOG CABIN DAYS OF ILLINOIS," ETC.

NEW YORK:
W. B. SMITH, & CO.,
BOND STREET.

TO

Every Friend of Liberty,

TO EVERY FRIEND OF HUMANITY,

TO EVERY HEART WHO HATH COMPASSION

FOR THE SORROWS AND MISFORTUNES OF MANKIND,

TO EVERY ONE WHO HATH CHARITY FOR OTHERS,

THIS BOOK IS MOST RESPECTFULLY INSCRIBED

BY THE AUTHOR.

ILLUSTRATIONS.

6

CONTENTS.

8   *CONTENTS.*

PREFACE.

·

Tyranny doth justice spurn,
Transforms a vase into an urn;
Thanks, that from the blood of hero slain,
Liberty springs to life again.

THE PEOPLE *vs.* THE KING.

THE Duke of Wellington cost England, in the shape of pay, pensions, etc., the sum of fourteen millions of dollars. The parliamentary returns of March 23, 1847, give the annual direct cost of royalty in England, the enormous sum of three millions eight hundred and forty-five thousand eight hundred and twenty-five dollars. The whole landed estate of England is in the hands of thirty thousand proprietors; Scotland, three thousand; Ireland, about six thousand. The lands belong to the aristocratic class, and are nearly exempt from taxation. In the report of 1847, the whole amount of land tax in Great Britain, was the sum of five millions nine hundred and fifteen thousand dollars, while the merchants, farmers, and the industrial classes, of every description, paid the sum of two hundred and forty-seven millions one hundred and sixty thousand dollars. In the above sum of money that is required to support royalty, there is an item of over one million of dollars for the private purse of the Queen.

A verse from the national song of England:

God save the king!
Send him victorious,
Soon to reign over us;
God save the king!

There are two chapters in the history of England that present two pictures. The one is full of joy, the other sorrow. The one relates that on the 19th of October, A. D., 1781, Lord Cornwallis, commander of the King's army, now engaged in suppressing the rebellion in

9

his majesty's American colonies, was compelled, by unavoidable accidents, to surrender the army to a certain rebel, called George Washington, assisted in his disgraceful disloyalty to his King, by a certain
Frenchman, called Lafayette. That was glad tidings to man; that
was the birth-day of the grandest Republic ever established for mankind. What a priceless inheritance is here transmitted to us, and in
our keeping for posterity. Let the toiling millions of our beloved
land remember, that it is far easier to lose liberty than to win it back
from the clutches of despotism, by revolution.

The other chapter is mournful. Napoleon, trusting to the generosity of the British nation, placed himself on an English vessel. On
his arrival, he asked of the prince regent the privilege of residing in
England, under the protection of their laws. He was not even allowed to land, or to have any communication with the people on
shore, but was banished, imprisoned on a small rocky island, far
away in the South Atlantic ocean.

In the year 1847, the land tax of France was one hundred and six-
teen millions of dollars, against five millions in England, the same
year. The industrial class of England paid a tax that year amount-
ing to the sum of two hundred and forty-seven millions of dollars.
While the industry of France paid only eighty-seven millions.

A verse from the French national anthem :

> "Oh Liberty, can man resign thee —
> Once having felt thy generous flame?
> Can dungeons, locks, and bars confine thee,
> Or whip thy noble spirit tame?
> Too long the world has wept, bewailing
> That Falsehood's dagger tyrants wield,
> But Freedom is our sword and shield,
> And all their arts are unavailing.
>> To arms! To arms! Ye brave.
>> Th' avenging sword unsheath.
>> March on, march on, all hearts resolved
>> On liberty or death."

May, A. D., 1800. It was in a high degree fitting that Napoleon
should have inaugurated his grand triumph in the cause of peace,
liberty and self-government in the very dawn of the nineteenth century. A century that up to 1879, has been marked by so many glorious achievements in civilization — crowned with many victories of

peace — marked improvement in all the branches of useful industry, laws, and government. The area of free thought and free speech has been vastly enlarged, with the almost universal recognition of the right of self-government in man.

The poet has given us new songs, filled with pathos, beauty, and grandeur. The architect, sculptor, and painter, have all given a new splendor even to their renascent work from the old masters of antiquity.

The crowned heads of England and Austria, with their nobles, and that unseen but omnipotent power behind the throne, well named the "almighty dollar," united together in a cruel, unjust, and unholy alliance, to crush out of France this glorious love of liberty and self-government.

In justice it should be said that the noble industrial classes of both England and Austria had no sympathy with these tyrannical acts perpetrated against France. But such are the crimes of despotism. The people are hopeless and helpless. This despotism not only exacts the fruits of toil, but demands the blood of their sons to maintain the thrice-accursed doctrine that God has appointed the king, to rule and rob.

England said to the American colonies, "accept a king." Patriotic hearts answered, —

> "The Star-Spangled banner, long may it wave,
> O'er the land of the free, and the home of the brave."

England and Austria said to France: "accept a Bourbon king;" and patriotic hearts answered: "To arms, to arms, ye brave; the avenging sword unsheath."

In March, 1879, when writing these lines, a correspondent of the "New York Herald" writes from Paris this, — "France has established a Republic. Paris is all ablaze with enthusiasm. Bands of Americans are parading the streets, singing the Star-Spangled Banner, while bands of Frenchmen are singing the Marseillaise."

It is grander by far to write the songs of a people, than to write their laws.

The foundation of all governments are the producing classes, and commerce that distributes the products of industry, either of hand or brain, to places where they are wanted. It matters not whether despotism springs from the royalty of kings, exacting almost countless

sums of money, to maintain its wanton extravagance, or from the
unjust exactions of a concentrated money power, it falls with crushing weight upon the shoulders of industry.

The well-to-do portion of the government foundation can endure
for some time, but the poorer classes of labor are soon driven to
despair. Then there is in the very vitals of the nation a smothered
and concealed volcano; a spark is communicated, then follows wide-
spread ruin and desolation. The despair that is produced by the
pangs of starvation knows no law.

In the spring of 1792 some French soldiers, who had determined
to strike for liberty, said this to one another, " We love France; we
will die for her; but where is the inspired one who can put our enthusiasm in glowing words to move the soul?" Little did they think
that in their very midst was the inspired one who would write the
song that would make his name immortal on earth.

Roget de Lisle, a soldier in the ranks, went to his chamber, and
there alone in the solitary midnight hour, sang to himself the grand
Marseillaise hymn, that moved the heart of every man that loved
human liberty with inspiration. Across the sea in our own land it
was answered with joy by our own inspired song of the " Star-Spangled Banner."

Six hundred brave men, half fed, half clothed, half armed, in the
revolution of '92, started from Marseilles and marched to Paris,
singing the grand hymn, confronted the armed legions of despotism,
accepted a glorious death in the cause of liberty with De Lisle's song
upon their lips.

There are times when despotism drives the friends of liberty to
despair, and the infernal is invoked.

Robespierre was the most mysterious character in French history.
The most of his life was spent in eloquent, stirring appeals in favor
of the merciful abolishment of the death penalty for all offences or
crimes. It is said, his writings and speeches were so brilliant and
powerful, that they gave him great prominence. What a ghastly ending
for such an exalted beginning. When in power, he caused the guillotine to run a stream of blood. The innocent perished with the guilty.
Friends perished with foe; decrepit old age and tender infancy died
together. To be suspected by the monster was to die. A peasant
girl was heard humming a song in praise of the Queen, and was put
to death.

The National Convention closed its blood-stained career forever. The reign of terror was ended. If France has shown great virtues, she has also been the theatre of great crimes. Her kings had been cruel to the children of the people. The people turned and put to death the children of the kings. In the name of liberty the Convention had committed countless crimes, clothed in the garb of virtue; the guillotine was the shrine of their idolatry. While the ensign of man's equality was unfurled in the halls of the Convention, the guillotine was behind the splendid image of liberty, where stood the executioner with axe in hand to put to death alike the guilty or innocent victims of his master. These scenes were too terrible to last. Mercy could no longer endure the sight of the tears of pleading innocence. The cry of anguish that went up from the stricken people was heard by the Infinite, and Robespierre, the grand central figure of this ghastly picture, fell a victim to the wrath of the fiend he had evoked. The National Convention had passed out of existence, the Council and Directory appeared in their stead, and in the horizon appeared the man of destiny standing at the portals of the nineteenth century with the avenging sword. The twilight of the eighteenth century laid Robespierre in the grave. The dawn of the nineteenth said to the grand captain of self-government, come. The close of the last century placed Robespierre on the guillotine. The beginning of the present placed Napoleon at the foot of the Alps with sixty thousand brave men to strike for peace and liberty, for their beloved France.

NAPOLEON.

The Council and Directory, now in power, organized three grand divisions of the army. The division that was to cross the Alps and conquer Italy was placed under the command of Napoleon. But recently the author was reading a description of Julius Cæsar. When he sought dominion he believed that he was led by destiny. He left behind him an exact account of his battles from day to day. These commentaries form a large fund of authentic history, and are universally admired for their elegance of style. He was courageous, self-possessed, clement, and generous. Although he was slender and delicate in make, he was able to make long marches, seldom stopped for repose — sleeping on the way in a litter or chariot. As a general he was equal to the greatest commander the world ever produced;

indeed there was no one that could hardly be compared to him, except, perhaps, Hannibal. As an orator he was second alone to Cicero. In his personal appearance he was commanding, with an open countenance, fair complexion, fine dark eyes, and said to be the handsomest man in Rome. I was forcibly impressed with the resemblance this picture bears to Napoleon. He believed that he was in the hands of destiny. His writings, his letters and orders, were universally admired for their brevity and force, also for their elegance of style. He was courageous, self-possessed, clement, and generous. He was slender in make, and never stopped in his marches for repose, sleeping on the way in his carriage. Indeed, I think it was said of him that he could sleep while sitting on his horse, and could sleep at any time he desired. As a general he has no equal in modern history; as an orator no man could utter great truths and splendid thoughts with more force and eloquence than Napoleon. In his personal appearance he was commanding, with an open countenance, fair complexion, fine large dark eyes, and was exceedingly handsome. There was this difference. Napoleon had a much grander field of action than Cæsar; his triumphs were by far more brilliant, and had a much greater effect on the destiny of man. He laid the foundation of a freedom of thought and speech that is destined, in the course of time, to redeem all Europe from despotism. One of the first acts of The Council of France, when placed in legislative power, was to propose peace with England and Austria, or otherwise to let France have peace, and the divine right of the people to establish for themselves a republican government. They refused to comply with this just demand. What untold, unnumbered blessings of peace, happiness, and prosperity would have been brought to the working classes of these three nations if this demand had been granted! At the close of the Napoleonic war, England had her people burthened with a tax of over four thousand millions of dollars, and millions of lives lost, the value of which cannot be measured by dollars and cents. For what? To make the workingmen of France accept a Bourbon for a king. Why did England and Austria want France to endure the despotism of a king? The answer is that France, under a republican government, with her great genius in all the departments of industry, would have been so prosperous, so happy, and the people so powerful in the triumphs of peace and liberty, that every throne and crown in Europe would be in danger from such a grand example of self-government. Thus it was that at the beginning of this century England and Austria taxed their workingmen money, and demanded of them the blood of their sons, to prevent the workingmen in France from enjoying the fruits of their own labor and the blessings of peace and liberty.

On the 6th day of May, 1800, an army of sixty thousand men were assembled at the foot of the Alps. They were to cross at three different points. Napoleon was with the main body of the army that crossed at the great St. Bernard. These soldiers were composed largely of Swiss and Alpine French mountaineers. Paul Lorraine was an adept in climbing the mountain cliffs; it was a part of his early education, — indeed, it was so with two-thirds of the entire force, — and hence the perfect success of this wonderful march, that astonished the civilized world with its brilliant intrepidity.

The Austrians, hearing for the first time of the ambitious designs of Napoleon to cross the Alps, treated it with scorn and contempt. The Swiss, the mountain French, and the highland Scotch are alike remarkable for their love of home and their love of liberty. They seem to love their homes for their dangers. Their hard struggles with a sterile soil gives them health, courage, and manhood. They breathe the free, pure air of the mountain cliffs, and look with disdain on those who dwell on the lowlands, as minions of arbitrary power and despotism. The terrors of the glacier and avalanche to them is enchantment. Go where they will, and their memory clings fondly to these mountain homes. The Highlander rushed proudly to the call of his chieftain to die in defence of the barren rocks. The Swiss in distant lands, in memory hears the melody of the Alpine horn, and the tears unbidden flow. Such an army with such a commander, and battling for such a cause was sure to triumph.

You would say to one of these soldiers, "Can you cross the Alps with those heavy guns, carriages, food, and ammunition? It is not possible!" He would say, "Why, it is nothing. See, we can go single along the glaciers, and most of the time double and treble; we will haul the guns on sleds, and pack the carriages on mules; we can carry some provisions; we will cut our pathway with axes out of the ice. If there comes a storm, and loosens the avalanche, or starts the glacier, probably we shall be lost." You would say again,

" When you get into Italy, you will meet the greatest army in Europe, veteran troops that have ever been victorious." He would say, " True, but we have conquered nature and the Alps, and surely now we need not fear man."

On the 16th of May the grand army broke forth with the strains of the Marseilles hymn, and the march commenced. Soon St. Pierre was reached and the road ended. Heroic band, march on, march on! You have with you the man chosen by destiny to vindicate the eternal principles of justice and liberty.

The Alps, monarch of the mystic realm, seated above the Olympic Jove of ancient days. To mortal man on earth's lower plains, thy throne is placed among the stars. What earthly king can vie with thee, in lofty, peerless majesty. How vast thy power! the dark abyss thy dungeon and thy prison keep. Thy army the mighty glacier that grinds to powder the massive granite hills. The ava-lanche that with one fell sweep could send armed battalions to an icy grave. Let loose the winds, the tempest, and the mountain storms; as well might man face the anger of Omnipotence. Mystic spirit of the mountain, around thy throne appears thy vast empire ! Ancient Rome still sitting on her hills — the throne of Cæsar van-ished. Sons of Rome still dwell amidst her vine-clad hills and fertile valleys, and her opulent cities, proud of ancient fame and historic memories. There is Greece, still mourning over fallen Athens and the tomb of Demosthenes. Far away in the distance rolls the waves of the classic sea that has borne on her bosom the commerce of forty centuries. There is the vast empire of the Czar, still waiting for the sick man's death, to grasp his Crescent crown. Here is dismembered Poland, still mourning for her exiled sons, and decking with flowers the tombs of her heroic dead. There the German, who in olden times crushed the grandest empire of antiq-uity. Yonder the islands of the proud Briton, mistress of the seas, forging chains for France. Here is chivalrous Spain ; she who dis-covered a new world ; and the land of the renowned Cid, the formi-dable foe of the powerful Moor. There is France pleading for peace and liberty. Cruelly she has been betrayed into the hands of her enemies. In olden times, when history commenced, Omnipotence rolled back the waves of the sea, and the children of Israel passed out of the land of bondage into the land of promise. The monarch of the mystic realm stayed the glacier, fastened the avalanche, bridged the abyss, silenced the storm; and the Man of Destiny passed unharmed in this march of triumph in the cause of liberty. It is not strange that Napoleon, like unto Cæsar, believed in destiny. That his fate was in the hands of some unseen, mysterious, power he could neither control or resist.

French Exiles of Louisiana.

Book I.

I.

Paul Lorraine.

In Provence, France, on the road from Digne to Briançon, well up towards the mountains, there is a little valley that has been occupied by a few families in succession, for generation after generation, for centuries. This remote and sequestered spot the traveller would name the Vale of Peace. Yet war had reached out its arm and grasped victims for carnage.

Jarvis Lorraine, an old resident, had fallen, while in the army of the Convention, at the siege of Toulon. Widow Lorraine is now dwelling with her son in that humble cottage by the road-side. It is flanked by a gentle, sloping hill, covered with a flourishing vineyard. The sun sets behind this hill, and there the first shadows of evening fall. The vines rejoice however, in the first beams of morning light, then they have the noonday sun. This is a good arrangement, as the culture of the vine requires above all things the sunlight, and plenty of fresh air to breathe. This keeps from the vineyard that terrible scourge, the black rot, and to a great extent the ravages of that parasite, the moth.

19

The cottage was covered with creepers and vines. Across the way was a small pasture field, where some cows, pigs, and sheep, were feeding on the rich pasture. Everything about this humble abode had the appearance of neatness and industry.

Mother Lorraine, as she was called, lived here with her son Paul, in apparent peace and contentment. The inhabitants of the valley, called her "mother" from the promptings of genuine affection.

This humble woman in lowly life, had an abiding faith in the goodness of the Infinite, and that in the end all would be well. The atheist, perched upon his intellectual throne, proud of his genius, and power to give even vice the appearance of virtue, would scoff at this faith — call it credulity, ignorance, superstition. Yet it cheered this poor woman in the hours of her greatest bereavement. To the most of those who may not trust in divine revelation, it is a mystery they cannot altogether grasp or comprehend. It found expression alike in the last hours of the great Webster, and the dying slave, when, afar off among the stars, he saw with faith a land of promise, where there was neither tears or bondage.

Not far from Mother Lorraine lived her brother-in-law Louis, enjoying about the same advantages in this world's goods as his brother's widow, with two sons to help him in the cares and labors of his place.

Across the road near the warbling mountain brook, that came down from the hill, was the home of Pierre Gerald and wife, with their daughter, Annetta. The top of the little cottage can just be seen over the spur of a sharp hill that springs out into the valley from the mountain.

This valley was the birthplace of Paul, and at the time
he was drafted in the army of the Alps he was about nine-
teen years of age. To have seen this peasant boy toiling
in the vineyard, with his homespun blouse, you never
would have dreamed that his life was to be one of such
strange events. He was everybody's friend. The children
of the valley looked upon him as a kind of divinity. A
little child slipped from the top of a steep crag, lodged
on the roots and limbs of a scraggy pine growing out
from the side of the ledge. What was to be done? The
cliff was a perpendicular rock two hundred feet from its
base to the place where the imperilled child was lodged.
Paul was called for consultation. Paul was of light build,
but strong, active, and muscular, noble hearted and full of
courage. He says, the child must be saved. His mountain
pick was in his hand. He passed up to the top of the hill
where the child had fallen. Soon, and the anxious ones who
had gathered there, — among the rest the mother of the child,
— looking up at the heroic youth so prompt to save the life
of her dear one, saw him strike his axe into the crevice of the
rock, swing down on a lower ledge, pass along some distance
from the object of the daring task. Again he returns on
a lower shelf of the rock, and is now standing immediately
beneath the child. Soon, and his mountain axe is fastened in the roots of the projecting tree; he draws himself
up, and the child is in the strong arms of the daring boy.
There was one in that assembly of anxious lookers-on,
that witnessed the event with as much joy as the mother
of the child. It was Annetta. Paul was her idol. A
smile of joy was on that sweet, pure face, so guileless and
innocent. She said, " Fear not for Paul, he is so good and
brave, surely no harm can come to him." A rope was

passed down to Paul, fastened around his waist, he threw his axe from him and was hauled up to the summit of the hill. The child was soon in the mother's arms. Heroic boy! How blessed for this world, were it filled with such hearts as thine!

At another time a horse ran away with a little boy, and was dashing furiously down the slope of the hill on the road. At the foot of the hill the road made a sudden turn to avoid a deep ravine. There was some little barrier to prevent accidents, but this little fellow was unable to control the horse so as to make the turn and avoid the precipice. Paul chanced to be near this bend in the road. He saw the terrible danger that threatened the life of the boy. He planted himself in front of the dashing animal, not far from the precipice. It appeared that the frightened brute was unable himself to change his headlong course from a direct one. It looked as if the horse would pass over Paul and trample him to pieces. When he came very near, Paul gave him a little berth, seized the boy, dragged him from his back, and the poor brute plunged over the railing and was dashed to pieces on the rocks below. Very many such events as this in the youthful days of this young hero gave him an enviable reputation for courage and intrepidity far beyond his companions and associates.

Paul and Annetta had grown up together here, in the purity, love, and happiness of Eden. They say history repeats itself; doubtless the sad story of Eden has been oft repeated. Peace, happiness, and contentment, destroyed by the wily serpent, bearing with it the knowledge of vain, idle pleasures, their allurements that lead to ruin and sorrow. It must have been such lives as Paul and

Annetta's that proved to the mind of the great writer on the law of evidence, Greenleaf, that the doctrine of absolute depravity, or natural depravity, was not to his mind proven. He says that a child tells the truth naturally, and is taught to lie; that truth is natural, lying artificial. The truth is easily told, and it is very hard to coin a falsehood that will pass current.

These children of nature grew together in virtuous simplicity, never dreaming that the wide world was full of crime, sorrow, and deceit; there was nothing in their thoughts they desired to conceal. They spoke to one another in the simple language of nature and truth. They worked together in the vineyard, and in the fields, dressed the vines, destroyed the weeds, and the parasites, worked among the flowers and vegetables, among the fruit-trees. Paul was an adept in pruning fruit-trees and grafting, and all the arts necessary to secure a good return for labor. They worked alternately on the Lorraine place and on the Gerald place. Annetta would have made a sorry figure in the gay, fashionable life of Paris. Yet, her heart, her mind, and that sweet smile that beamed forth from her kind, quiet face, was full of grandeur.

Paul would say to Annetta, " I love you as I love the flowers."

" Why Paul ? "

" Because they are so beautiful, so pure, like the angels my dear mother talks about."

Annetta would say, " I do love you so."

" Why, Annetta ? "

" Because, Paul, you are so good, and brave, and kind."

Oftentimes she would see Paul pass along the verge of the rocky cliff with the agility of a mountain chamois.

She would say to herself, " I love him so, he is so brave."
Then Paul's constant care and attention to the old people
in the valley was so considerate and generous, that he was
endeared to every one. As Paul grew older he became
more thoughtful, and at times there was a sad tone to
his voice — perhaps he was thinking of his father killed in
battle at the siege of Toulon, or perhaps the day was near
when he would be required to leave his dear mother,
Annetta, and the children of the valley.

Annetta would say to him, " If you go from us, you
will surely come back to us, for you are so good and
brave, no harm can come to you."

" Yes, but Annetta, the good often suffer. Sometimes
we hear of the brave being put to death unjustly, and
I may be killed in battle."

" Yes," Annetta replied to him, " the good do often
suffer, but not long ; the good angels find them out and
lead them forth into the sunlight and happiness, and then
courage will oftentimes save your life in battle."

Paul was cheered with the words of this little philoso-
pher, arguing in her simple way of the power there was to
protect him from evil, by using the armor of virtue and
courage. He was thinking that when he was climbing the
lofty hills, passing over the snow-clad glacier or the brow
of the avalanche, that without firmness and courage he
would have been oftentimes dashed into the abyss.

" Annetta," he would say, " I may go into the army and
fall in the battle-field."

" If you die in the battle, fighting for our dear France,
how I would love your memory, Paul ; but I would not
live long. I would not cry or mourn, but I would feel as
if severed from earth, and, like the vine severed from its

root, fade, wither, and perish. I would die and go to
you, Paul; for surely the good God would have you in his
keeping."

"But, Annetta, I would have you live and take care of
our dear old parents and the children in the valley. But —
well, well, Annetta, we will not talk of these sad events. I
believe I will come back to you safe and well, and I will
love you all the better, and together we will take good care
of our parents and the little children, dress the vines,
climb the hills, gather fruit. and take good care of our
cows and sheep; and in the twilight-hour sing our beautiful songs and be so happy."

At night they would sit in the cottage door and gaze
upon the stars, and wonder at their beauty and the cause
of their creation. There was one star that they had selected for their future home. When at eve it sparkled in
the west, it received their united love and adoration.

Paul's educational advantages were limited, but, like his
race, both ancient and modern, his perceptions were quick.
The Lorraine family, many years before this period, had
been successful merchants of Marseilles. Misfortune, perhaps, drove this branch of the family into this remote
place. There were some old Greek and Roman books
translated into French, from which Paul had drawn a considerable fund of knowledge. All he knew of Napoleon
was from hearsay, and Napoleon lost nothing, in stature or
greatness, from the bright fancy of this French peasant.

The hour that formed the turning point in the strange
life of this interesting boy had been sounded. He was
ordered to join Napoleon's army, congregated at the foot
of the Alps, at the Great St. Bernard pass. He was prepared, for he expected it. He was clothed in the garb of

a French soldier; was to leave his kind mother, Annetta, Uncle Louis, and the dear little children of the valley. His good mother felt sad over this parting. Sorrow for the death of Paul's father had left its bitter memory. Yet she bore up against these sorrows with that strong faith and assurance that God was good, and in the end would make all well. To her this faith was an impenetrable shield.

Annetta was pale and tearless. Her faith was in her idol. She said this : "I know he is good and brave. Surely he will not be harmed by any one. Who could harm such a one? So kind to all."

Annetta, Uncle Louis, and the children followed with Paul far on the way of his departure, and then gazed after him until a bend in the road carried him out of sight. It is the first act in his dramatic life. He turned and gazed upon the dear scenes of his childhood. How his heart did cling to the beloved spot, so full of sweet memories. His life had been happy there in his home, for it had been natural and truthful. To him it was a grand picture. On one side the Alps towered up in the sky in majesty and grandeur, its bosom veiled in the purest white, its summit with its pinnacles, walls, and battlements, with their deep purple shadows and golden lights from the rising sun. At its base long lines of dark green forests at intervals ran out into the valley then swept high up to the foot of some tall, rocky cliff, again rolled off into distance and was lost to sight. There was the cottage home, the winding brook, still warbling along with its cheerful song, the little fields and vine-clad hills, the winding road to Briançon, above all, the loving hearts in those humble abodes. The objects in this world that are dear or pleasing to the eye, are vastly more precious to us when we are about to part with them or lose them. Your dear friend is on his death-bed. How much dearer he is to you in the last hour. You forget his faults; and his virtues are unfolded to your sight with additional splendor. Go where you will, brave boy, and the picture of yonder valley and the loved ones who dwell there will cling to your memory. The impression will be as vivid and as bright as if traced in line and coloring by the hand of the Infinite.

Annetta to him was a beautiful being of dream-land. His mother, who had been, in the long years gone by, the personification of loving kindness, rose up at parting a being possessing far more excellence than anything on earth. To him his good mother possessed something akin to divinity. When she parted with him she laid her hand upon his head and said, —

"Paul, my son, God will bless you for my sake."

These words he believed. He believed that his mother was merely a link between him and the unseen world. The passing winds sighed to him a gentle, mournful farewell — he is gone.

The night followed the day. The landscape smiled. The mountain brook still warbled its song. The birds filled the valley with charming melody. The sun poured its golden light down upon the peaceful valley. All unconscious of the sad hearts, throbbing in these cottage homes — of the humble peasants.

II.

PAUL'S departure, was as if a shadow had fallen on this happy valley, and saddened every heart.

Annetta came often to see Mother Lorraine, and comfort her in the hours of sorrow; and together, they talked fondly of the absent one so dear to them.

Annetta loved to recall the many incidents that marked Paul's faithful, loving disposition.

His life was a part of her life, for they were like two beautiful, tender flowers, that had budded, and bloomed into fragrance and beauty on the same stem.

The mother was doubtless resting on that promise that flashed upon the cross at Calvary. All the sorrows of this world could not make her for one moment waver in her sublime faith. (I have no reasoning to offer, no logic to bring forward, to prove that this faith was not well founded. I will not undertake to argue with the atheist or the infidel. If Divine Revelation is a failure, this mysterious quality of the human heart is beyond our grasp and comprehension. All I can do is to record the fact that this woman's whole life was a mission of love, and self-denial.)

Mother Lorraine sacredly preserved every thing that would bring to memory her son. In a little closet she had his wooden shoes, his home-spun blouse, and his hat, that he wore in his hours of toil — now cast off, to be exchanged for the dress of the soldier of France. How good would it be for this world if the rulers of kingdoms, and governments, would walk in the same paths of honor and rectitude, as followed by the feet that filled those wooden shoes. How grand would it be if the robes of state always covered a heart as full of love, charity, and mercy, as had throbbed under that faded blouse. Oh, that kings, monarchs, and presidents, were as willing to give to honest toil, the fruits of industry, as he who wore that hat, *instead of* kingly crown.

BOOK II.

I.

MARENGO.

PAUL LORRAINE was in the army of Napoleon. His training as a mountaineer rendered his service in the march across the Alps of great importance. There was no peculiar quality in the most humble soldier in the ranks that ever escaped the quick observation of Napoleon.

Paul's agility and intrepidity in climbing the rocky cliffs, his ready use of the mountain pick, in cutting pathways in the glaciers, his sound, good judgment, in the choice of proper passages for footmen and mules, was soon a matter of observation, and he requested that Paul should keep near the guide who led the mule upon which he was seated, and direct him in his course, and make the pathway more secure. On one occasion Napoleon said to Paul, "What is your name?" He answered promptly, "Paul Lorraine." "Ah, it is a good name, and if my memory serves me rightly, belongs to Marseilles. Where are you from, my young friend?" "From Provence, sire; not far from Briançon. My father's name was Jarvis Lorraine, sire, and fell in the seige of Toulon."

Napoleon replied promptly, "Lorraine, and fell at Toulon. Ah, then you have lost your best friend in behalf of France, and all that is left to you is your mother?" "Yes, sire, that is a good deal left; my mother is the kindest of women. She thinks that God requires her to make these sacrifices in favor of her country, that is so deeply injured and wronged by other nations; and she daily asks God to protect France and her defenders."

" I know, brave youth, that you love your good mother; have you no other friends?"

" Yes, sire; my good Uncle Louis, and Annetta."

" Ah, Annetta; who is this Annetta?"

" Annetta Gerald, sire."

" She is more than a friend to you, Paul, I am thinking?"

" Yes, sire, I love Annetta; I love her for her virtues. She is kind and good to every one."

This plain, candid admission of his love for Annetta, without the least desire to conceal the secret of his heart, and not the least show of false modesty, was very pleasing to Napoleon.

" I need not ask you, Paul, if Annetta loves you?"

" Yes, sire, she loves me well; and at our parting she said I surely would come back to her, for no harm could come to the good and the brave; and said I might fall in the battle-field, but if I fell in defence of France my memory would be very dear to her."

" Paul, whenever you want a friend apply to me."

Paul started off on some duty he had to perform; and this tete-a-tete was closed. It had a very visible effect on Napoleon, and doubtless the conclusion in his mind was that France, possessing such mothers, daughters, and sons, would surely triumph over her enemies, and in the end achieve peace and liberty; that surely the Infinite would hear the prayers of these earnest souls calling for help in the hour of their tribulation.

The army is passing the hospital of the great St. Ber-

nard. The good monks, refresh long lines of soldiers as
they pass, with bread, cheese, and wine. The hospital of
St. Bernard is creditable to humanity. The good monks
pass their days in this wild, wierd solitude, to minister unto
suffering men, acts of mercy and charity. It is a grand
picture in life's weary way. Good is it that there are men
willing to dwell in this bleak, dreary, and desolate abode ;
listen to the howling storm and the wintry winds ; go forth
into the rushing tempest of ice and snow to save the dying stranger, warm him into life, and say to him, thou hast
paid us ; for charity pays him that gives, as well as him that
receives. And there, too, the noble dog of St. Bernard,
goes forth amid the pelting storm and rushing winds, at
the midnight hour, amidst the terrible danger of rock,
glacier, and avalanche, with unerring instinct, finds some
poor human soul who is dying far away from the loved
ones of home and kindred, takes him and bears him along
through snow and ice, along the rocky bridge, past the
abyss, places him in the hands of his kind master, and
could he speak would say, "warm him into life. I found
him perishing and in pity I brought him to you to save."
Thus this brute is trained to acts of kindness that would
add grandeur to the noblest acts of man. Far back in my
early schoolboy days, the recital of the deeds of self-
denial, and the noble acts of these men of mercy and
charity, and the faithful dog of St. Bernard formed a bright,
beautiful picture in my heart of man's charity for man,
that has clung to my memory bright and glowing through
all the long years of my life. The good monks blessed
the soldier as he marched on with heart resolved on liberty
or death. The soldier thanked the good monk and the
Infinite blessed them both.

Paul Lorraine was still prompt and active in the discharge of duty. His superior skill in mountain life was pretty much recognized by all. Oftentimes he was sent forward as a pioneer to determine the most practical pathway. Most of his time was occupied in the immediate front of Napoleon, who seemed to rely strongly on the sound judgment of this youthful soldier in determining courses, and his ready skill in the use of the mountain pick in cutting pathways.

The valley of Aosta is reached ; a long, narrow chasm, through which the river Aosta rushes with violent force barely leaving a pathway on the side for a horseman. Precipitous cliffs hundreds of feet high, rose up on either side like lofty prison walls, defying mortal man to scale their giddy heights. All at once consternation and dismay was expressed on the face of the soldier. A lion was in the pathway. In the very centre of this narrow valley was a lofty pinnacle of rock inaccessible on the side the army was approaching. On the top of this rock was the fort of Bard, with cannon placed in position that commanded the valley, through which Napoleon's army was advancing. Was this the end of all this triumphant achievement in crossing the Alps with this army and its heavy munitions of war? Napoleon saw the peril instantly, and passed to the front. With great difficulty and danger he clambered on the side of the rugged rocks, concealing himself by the stunted trees and bushes, until he got above the fort, and could see down into it. He had a full view of the cannon in position and the men in the fort, ready to use them when the proper time came. He was looking for a position for his artillery to send a plunging shot into the fort, and dismantle it. This was among the impossibles. On a high eminence, beyond the fort, there was plainly visible a road winding in the hills. If his army could only reach that road it was possible for him to pass, without the guns of the fort being able to interfere with his march. Napoleon returned and stated to Paul what he had seen on the distant hills, and asked him to find a pathway from this valley into the road. Paul promptly answered, " I can try, sire, and with your permission will undertake it." His mountain pick was in his hand. He crossed the rushing waters of the Aosta, with the aid of a rope in the hands of soldiers, passed along down the stream on the opposite side and came back on a projecting ledge, until he was far above the heads of the army in the valley, and gave them to understand that the many shots that had been fired at him from the fort, had passed him unharmed. The brave boy dashed on up the cliff, until he stood on the very summit, and there he saw the road Napoleon had observed, and that descended to the village of Aosta, in Piedmont, and also back towards the hills, on the line of march which the army had been passing; and thus, by returning he discovered a pathway, that they might in safety reach this road. He reported to Napoleon, and under cover of the night the army passed the fort, without the least injury. The Austrian commander of Fort Bard, reported that the army of Napoleon, had passed in the night, but without any artillery, as it was impossible for him to move his guns on a narrow pathway upon which a mule could scarcely walk. The army in Piedmont, the wonderful march is accomplished.

It is truly said, that he who has justice with him is doubly armed. This army represented what is generally called in all countries the middle classes of France. They are the vitality of all people, and are in sympathy with the lower classes, and protect them from the effects of despotism to a great extent. This class in France are people of a high degree of intelligence. They had seen from the experience of centuries, that the old governments of Europe, hereditary kings supported by an extravagant, wanton and corrupt nobility, could never bring peace and prosperity. They knew that if France was left to act for herself, she could establish and maintain a republican government. Never was there a grander achievement in the cause of justice and self-government, than the triumphant march of Napoleon across the Alps.

II.

DESAIX.

THE Battle of Marengo occurred June 14, 1800. All battle-fields leave tragical memories. Marathon, Bunker Hill, and Marengo are each marked with a mournful, pathetic history. Each called forth a nation's tears, mourning for heroic sons, who had fallen in a struggle with despotism and defending liberty. Marathon had Cynegirus; Marengo, Desaix; Bunker Hill had Warren. They arise up to memory out of these sepulchres, sanctified to human liberty, clothed with a radiant glory, grander by far than any honor earth can bestow. At the battle of Marengo, for some time it was as if these brave men had passed the horrible dangers of the mountain march, had endured hardships in every conceivable form, in vain. That they had encountered all this suffering but to find a grave upon the plains of Italy. The charge after charge

of the trained soldiers of Austria was terrible; nothing
but the most heroic courage saved the defenders of France
from quick destruction. Desaix was anxiously expected
with reinforcements. Napoleon sat upon his horse with
that inexpressible serenity that seemed to say, I see the
end, and it is victory. The French army were as if struggling in the last effort for supremacy on the battle-field, as
if saying, can it be that the cause of liberty is to perish
here? Then a moment of supreme anxiety, verging on
despair; but destiny decreed that France should triumph.
Hark! there is floating on the air a dull booming sound,
like distant thunder. Thousands of tongues shouted the
name of Desaix! Desaix! It was the cannon of Desaix
announcing glad tidings. Napoleon said of him, Desaix
is of the heroic mould of antiquity. He will decide this
contest on the side of justice and liberty. He rapidly
moves along in solid column, and passes on to the field of
battle. The Austrian is dismayed. Rapid, still more
rapid were the blows this athlete of war struck the serried
ranks of despotism. The whole entire army of peace and
liberty, with hearts renewed and resolved, charged upon
the Austrian army; they wavered, broke into fragments, and
at last gave away, and the victory was with Napoleon.
To France this is a national sepulchre, sacred to the memory of the heroic dead. Marengo has a history full of
mournful pathos. Had you have asked a French soldier
about Marengo, with tears he would have told you that
Desaix came to conquer and to die. That the cannon in the
distance that brought joy to other hearts, was but the
mournful funereal knell of the man who came to conquer
and to die. Had you have asked a Greek in olden times
about Marathon, he would have told you the sad, mournful

story of Cynegirus, who after performing wondrous deeds of valor in the field of Marathon, was disarmed and cruelly slain by Persians, while rushing to save Athens from the invader.

Ask the American to tell you about the battle of Bunker Hill. With touching pathos he would relate to you how the noble Warren went to the front of battle and said, " I am ready to die, if liberty can live, and have a resting-place in the new world." The victory of Marengo placed Italy in the hands of Napoleon. The dawn of the nineteenth century witnessed the advent of the second Cæsar into Imperial Rome.

Paul Lorraine had been seriously wounded in the battle. He fought side by side with a good, brave youth like himself, Jean Gendron. When Paul fell wounded and disabled, with the loss of blood, from a severe wound in the head and musket-ball in the arm, Jean dragged or carried him to a place of security, procured surgical aid and had his wounds properly cared for. As Jean was no longer wanted in the battle-field, he stayed with his friend until rest and refreshments had brought him to a knowledge of his situation. For some time he was unconscious. The last incident that had clung to his memory was the joyful shout that "Desaix was coming," and hearing the distant sound of his cannon. The surgeon pronounced his wounds serious, but not decidedly dangerous. When his mind was returned, he thanked his friend Jean for his constant care and kindness. The first thought that entered his mind was his love for his dear old mother and Annetta. He thought of the words that had comforted him so much in his hours of danger. " If you fall in defence of France, your memory will be so dear to me. The good and true never remain long in misery and distress; the good angel soon finds them and leads them out of the shadows of misfortune into the glad sunlight of happiness and joy."

Upon further examination of Paul's condition, the surgeon reported that it would be a long time before he would be again in a condition for service in the army, and by a special order from Napoleon himself, he was well supplied with means, and sent to his happy, peaceful home in the valley on the Briançon road.

Little did Annetta or Paul think that the first time the shadows of misfortune would fall upon him, Annetta herself would be the sweet angel to bring the sunlight of joy to his heart. Well will it be for him, if, in the dark hours of tribulation, in the years to come, his noble soul, stricken with agony and despair, God will, in tender compassion, send this same angel of love and mercy, to lead him out of the shadows of misfortune, into the sunlight of joy.

Book III.

I.

Italy.

Leghorn is situated on the Mediterranean sea, and is the principal seaport of Tuscany, not far from Pisa and Florence, the famous seat of art. There in Florence originated the Florentian school, and the illustrious name of Leonardo da Vinci. Here, too, is the poetic Valley of Arno.

One of the main features of the excellence of the old masters in art was in the management of shadows in the background. The Chinese form some very good foreground pictures, both in landscape and figure painting, yet they seem to have had no conception of the superior advantage in perspective and background shadows. The old masters with Leonardo da Vinci in a very high degree displayed wonderful skill in detaching the front figures from the shadows. These background shadows were not of any distinct color; there is in fact no color that the eye can detect. The colors with which these shadows are formed are so blended, and laid on the convass, that the eye is deceived into the conclusion that you are looking through the shadows on more distant objects, while the foreground figures rise up in front detached from both shadow and object.

There are separate photographs taken of the different personages represented in Da Vinci's painting of the "Last Supper," and any person well versed in the character of the disciples can readily tell the one which each figure was intended to represent. Any one could select Judas. This arises from the fact that the artist, it is said, selected corresponding characters, as near as possible from living models.

In the fore part of the present century, in the city of Leghorn, not very far distant from the gate leading to Pisa, there is a mansion (or palace, as the Italians call any large edifice) belonging to a family by the name of Vilani, connected with an old aristocratic family of Florence, and was at this time occupied by Count Vilani, Lady Verono, and a quiet, retired looking man, with the appearance and dignity of a priest, whose name was Alonzo. It was generally understood that the family of Vilani was connected with the celebrated family of the Medici through the forefathers of Lady Verono and Alonzo. These children of nobility are very numerous throughout the Italian states, for the reason that titles of nobility descend to all the sons of the family. They all like a life of splendid ease. They detest hard work, and the largest portion of them are driven to the very extremes of poverty.

The property descends to the sons, and is hereditary, and cannot be sold, and thus you will often find a marquis, renting out to strangers furnished apartments in his palace, while he has a little shop in the basement, where he sells oil, wine, olives, fruits, etc. An American marquis would naturally take to the peanut trade. To an American count the pop-corn commerce would be most admirable. A duke, the head and front of a first class saloon! It is not strange to see in Italy a real, genuine marquis or count, begging for food or clothing. How strange it would appear in our country to have a real marquis go to the back door of the kitchen department, say to the lady of the house, "Something to eat, I am hungry."

She says, "I will give the noble marquis to understand that he must first weed the garden, hoe the potatoes, and clean the front yard, then his lordship shall no longer hunger for food."

"Madame, what is all this; why it is work, and my ancestors would rise from their graves were I to use the shovel, hoe, or spade. Good-day, Madame."

Or, "Noble duke, how is the pop-corn trade?" or, "My lord count, is the peanut trade lively?" In our hotels the drummers of commercial houses would have the titled nobility to serve them at the table — dukes, marquises, and counts, to obey their orders. It would be a little inconvenient to be using these sounding titles, but it would pay in dignity. It would sound well to say, "Noble Duke some warm potatoes;" or, "Count, hand me a glass of water. Marquis! bottle wine, napkins, glasses, quick!" Finally, with a great deal of gusto, you order the marquis to black your boots.

This reminds me of an artist of some prominence, but exceedingly vain and self-conceited, who said to Governor Ford, of Illinois, "I am well convinced, governor, that gentlemen who are distinguished for talent and genius, even in republican democratic Illinois, should be distinguished by some title."

"Well," said the governor, "I am willing, and as governor of Illinois, I will commence on you."

"Well, what title would you confer on me, governor."

"Count Jackaski."

Governor Ford was never afterwards importuned on the question of a titled nobility.

Those Italian counts and marquises who turn their hereditary palace into some practical use, and thus earn an honest livelihood, are a vast improvement on their ancestors, who lived in splendid ease and luxury on the earnings of others' toil and industry, and who formed a class of nobility who gave strength, power, and endurance, to an organized system of robbery, and plunder, of the toiling masses, and with cruel mockery called this heartless system a government. If the people complain they say, "kings are divinely appointed to rule over you, and you have no choice but to obey."

II.

The Insane Count.

With this Count Vilani there was a serving man, an Italian, who went by the name of Geno, a most villainous model of humanity. Surely no one could ever recover damages against Geno for obtaining goods under false pretences. To look at his face you would think of the sign you often see at places where intruders are not wanted, "look out for the dog." Da Vinci surely must have met one of Geno's ancestors and took him for a model of his Judas in the last supper.

These were the principal members of the household of Count Vilani. They were, so to speak, the foreground figures of the picture. In the background there were shadows filled with vague images of injustice, like the dark shadows of Benjamin West's painting of "Death on the Pale Horse," filled with indistinct images of terror. To the outside

world there was a cloud over the house of Vilani, arising
from vague and undefined hints of crime, that never had
assumed any direct or specific charge of acts committed
by any member of this household that the law would recognize or seek to punish. Count Vilani had a cousin,
Francisco Vilani, who had become heir to a considerable
fortune. He was insane, and was for some time confined
in an institution for the insane, at Florence.

This Count Vilani, or Colonel Vilani, as he was sometimes called from his having served some years in the
army, had by his influence, and position, induced the
public authority to place his cousin Francisco, under his
charge, and urging the change upon the ground that he
could be better cared for under the immediate attention
and supervison of his relatives, Lady Verono, Alonzo, and
himself, they being the only relatives the unfortunate
Francisco had living. The insane cousin did not, however,
long survive the change. He gradually passed away to
his grave.

Soon gossip began to weave its dismal tales of slow
poison, or starvation, in a dungeon in the palace, and that
a vast amount of gold, diamonds, and precious stones,
were concealed and hid away in some secret place to be
used by the perpetrators of the crime. Colonel Vilani, of
course, accounted to the authorities for the property of the
deceased, but gossip would say, "shame! shame!"

These tales, of course, soon passed away, and their
memory forgotten, leaving nothing but a very indistinct
impression on the public mind that something of the kind
was some years ago talked about among idling gossips.

Colonel Vilani was of fine, personal appearance, haughty
and elegant in deportment, tasty and fashionable in dress

There was one conclusion that any one would arrive at,
that there was a cold, sinister expression in his face, that
stamped him as a vain, heartless man. He was accused
of being a libertine,— and surely the expression of his face
was that of gross sensuality, — and that these charges were
founded on facts. But a nobleman in any part of Italy,
with plenty of gold to back his title and claim to nobility,
would be invincible against any charges of this character,
from the populace ; and Colonel Vilani could indulge himself in all his licentious acts with perfect impunity.

III.

LADY VERONO.

LADY VERONO, thus living with Count Vilani, her relative, alone apparently, in the palace, did not necessarily
involve her in any suspicion of improper conduct. It was
not unusual for relatives among the nobility, thus to live
together in family residences. Why she was called Lady
Verono, history does not inform us. Verono was her
family name, and she was regarded as the lady of the
palace household.

To the casual observer, this beautiful woman, with her
graceful suavity, and polished address, challenged admiration and affection. This splendid medallion had a reverse
side that was terrible. Here was one of the marked traits
of the house of Medici. The accomplished artist would
fondly trace those classic features upon the canvass, and
view his work with delight and admiration. Yet, when he
went away from the subject and his easel, a shadow would

fall on his heart, producing a vague, undefined terror. In his imagination there would arise the dim outline of a fiend clothed in the garb of beauty and loveliness. Perhaps the beautiful evil one that carried the poisoned chalice into Paradise, was such a being, to have beguiled Eve, so that she cast from her peace and happiness, and was led into the paths of sin, to suffer the bitter pangs of woe. Lady Verono was a lady of marked talent, ability, and energy, and doubtless was the master spirit in the household.

Annetta, the humble peasant girl of the Alps valley in France, was beautiful, because her heart was good and pure. She was loved, for her soul was true and lofty, and full of grand thoughts and emotions, and because her faith rested in an infinite God, who to her was the personification of goodness, mercy, and love. Her humble garb and plain features added splendor to these charms.

Alonzo, the other prominent member of this Vilani household, was not a marked character, judging from his personal appearance. He had a quiet look, and was retired in his habits, and seldom in public. He had been educated for the priesthood, and why he did not fulfil his holy calling we cannot say. He was a relative of the family of Vilani; how, or in what degree, the writer is unable to state.

This palace or mansion was erected after the style of the buildings in Florence ; erected more with regard to durability than the classic style of architecture.

The interior was furnished with costly elegance. The carpetings, hangings, and tapestry, of the most expensive material; paintings representing events in the lives of the apostles ; family portraits of members of the Vilani family, who had been laid in the vault at Florence, centuries ago ; beautiful landscapes of picturesque Italy, by Salvator Rosa, decorated the lofty walls of the apartments. Here and there were choice pieces of sculpture, marked with the genius of Angelo.

On one side of this edifice there was a verandah, adjusting itself to the projecting angles. The first story had the appearance of dead walls, while the second story in front was embellished with a splendid, lofty portico, looking out upon the blue waters of the Mediterranean Sea.

A wide area of cultivated ground surrounded the palace, and was walled in with stone, archways, and hanging-gates of iron at the entrances. The building was marked with the age of centuries, and was doubtless erected long before the struggle between Pisa and Florence, when the chained harbor of Pisa was broken by the Florentians.

It was generally understood that the family of Vilani, were connected by kindred blood with the Medici of Florence, and that this relationship came by the ancestors of the Lady of Verono.

The founders of this very remarkable family of Medici were practitioners of medicine in Florence. Its history begun, however, with Cosmo de Medici, born in 1389, who became the head and principal in a commercial establishment, that had a counting-house in every commercial city of any importance at that period, and was said to be the richest man in all Europe. He was generous, humane, and enterprising, and during his time the Florentines enjoyed the highest degree of prosperity and happiness. But this vast wealth laid the foundation for a royal family, whose career was marked with tyrannical cruelty and

crime, connected with talent, ability, and energy, unsurpassed. They added glory and renown to Florence, but
soon overturned the republican government, and established a despotism. Catherine de Medicis, the mother
of Charles the IX. of France, was a descendant of Cosmo
de Medeci, and through her son, while in his minority,
ruled France with a reign of terror. The historian says
of her that she was distinguished alike for great talents
and great cruelty. The history of this family furnishes
a valuable lesson to the friends of liberty and self-government : That the concentration of vast money power, in
the hands of a few designing men, is one of the most
deadly enemies to the peace, prosperity, and liberty, of the
people.

IV.

THE FLOWER GIRL.

OUTSIDE of the walls there are small farms or gardens
rented or leased to peasants, who are very industrious and
thrifty. They cultivate the vine, olive, delicious fruits of
all kinds, and vegetables for the city market. The daughters and wives of these gardeners may be seen passing
into the different gates of Leghorn dressed in their picturesque style, with baskets on their heads, ladened with the
rich products of the garden and vineyard.

Not far from the Pisga gate, on the hill-side, there was
at this period, an old man, his wife and daughter, dwelling
in a cottage and engaged in cultivating a small vineyard
with fruits of various kinds, flowers, and vegetables.
They were industrious, prosperous and frugal. The old
man and his wife were skilled in gardening and in the cul-

tivation of rare flowers. They had emigrated here from
some part of Greece years back, and were generally known ·
by the name of the Greek gardeners, and Iphi, their
daughter, had no other name than Iphi the flower girl.
The daughter, being called Iphi, was probably an abbrevi-
ation of Iphigene, that lovely virgin represented in a
beautiful work of art, when about to be sacrificed to
appease the anger of Diana. The goddess relented when
she saw her beauty, innocence, and tears, and placed a
kid upon the altar of sacrifice instead, and carried Iphigene away from earth and consecrated her to Vesta.

The ancient Iphigene was not more lovely, though represented by the bright conception of artistic genius, than
this modern Iphigene, the humble daughter of the gardener at Leghorn. Iphi possessed the classic beauty of
Verono, and the chaste, pure soul of Annetta.

The humble garb of the flower girl added charms to
her graceful form, while her innocence and sweetness of
temper beamed forth in every word and action.

Iphi was at this period, being four years since the battle
of Marengo, about the age of fourteen or fifteen, and had
been, for several years back, actively engaged in carrying
fruit and flowers to the market of Leghorn.

Among her constant customers was Lady Verono, who
had impressed her with the idea that she was everything
that was good and true. Oftentimes she would say to her
parents, "How kind, how good the lady of the palace is to
me. She oftentimes presses me to take more than I ask
for my flowers."

Thus it was that Iphi's life was a life of peace, love, and
gratitude. What joy to her to provide for her dear father
and mother, who had so kindly watched over her in her

tender years of infancy. Alas, for us poor mortals! these
dreams of happiness vanish. The sad story of Eden is
constantly repeating its woe. That beautiful fiend that
led Eve away from peace and happiness, is still abroad in
the world with the poisoned cup, pressing it to the lips of
virtue and innocence.

There was at this time a Louis Dejon, the son of a
neighboring gardener, who at times kindly assisted Iphi
and her parents, working in the garden and vineyard. As
Louis is connected with this narrative, even to its final
denouement, it would not be out of the way to say a few
words in his description.

He was more than an ordinary person, although the son
of a peasant. He was one of those characters you will
sometimes see, who are stumbling-blocks to the teachers of
phrenology and physiognomy. His face was expressionless. In person he was short, thick-set, strong and muscular. His deportment reserved. When he spoke it was
rather sensible, firm, and resolute. If a dishonest man
wished his services to perpetrate some scheme of villainy,
Louis could make him believe he had his man, by his resolute, firm avowals, and nothing in his looks to deny his
words. There was nothing in his appearance attractive,
nor was there anything repulsive. To see him, he was
nothing; to know him was everything. His perceptions
were strong and quick, a genuine heart, with dauntless
courage.

About this period, there was a garrison established
at Leghorn, with several regiments of troops, stationed
there in readiness for any emergency that might arise
demanding their service. When Napoleon became the
master of the Italian states, his policy was reconcilia-

tion. They claimed him as an Italian, and not a Frenchman. Very many of them were like the peasant woman of the Alps, who said to him, " Sire we are willing to change kings — you will be the king of the people — not the king of the nobles." His policy was rather to break down all discrimination of Italian or French, and thus in the end make all Italy French. Thus it was that Col. Count Vilani was made commander of the garrison at Leghorn. His power was local, and upon the removal of troops his authority ceased. In one of these regiments was Jean Gendron, who had saved Paul Lorraine's life at Marengo, by carrying him off the field of battle, procuring for him surgical assistance in time to save his life.

Jean was a smart, good-looking, clever man ; a true, faithful friend ; a good soldier ; always ready and willing to aid a friend ; prompt and active in the discharge of every duty. He became acquainted with Louis Dejon, and through Louis, he first saw Iphi, and was at first sight enraptured with her rare beauty, and cheerful, joyous, happy disposition. Iphi also liked Jean, with his open, frank kindness, and cheering words, so that Iphi said of him, " He appears so friendly, and pleasant, that Louis, I must say, I like your friend very much."

Jean was oftentimes stationed at the garrison gates as guard, and Iphi in her daily duty of attending market, passed this way, as there was a short street going out into the market way from the avenue coming down from the Pisa gate.

Jean would salute her in terms of tender affection, rest her for a while of her burdens, and speak to her cheerful words.

Iphi would say : " Ah, Jean, you are so good and kind,

I know very well you are a true friend, and will not desert
me. Jean do you know that I sometimes think there is
trouble coming to me, and it makes my heart sad; and yet
I cannot tell what it is or where it is to come from. I am
so happy with my dear father and mother, and every one
seems kind to me; Lady Verono is such a beautiful lady,
and so good, that sometimes I think my happiness is too
great to last."

Jean says, "The Lady Verono is the person who lives
in the commander's palace."

"Yes, Jean, that is the person I mean; she is very
good to me."

"I dare say," replied Jean, "but, Iphi, the world is not
what it seems. You judge others by your own pure motives,
kind heart, and warm affections. I cannot see any motive
the Lady Verono could have in injuring so innocent a one
as you. Yet, Iphi, vice often accomplishes its purpose, by
using the credulity of innocence."

"Jean, dear Jean," she said, "when these sad thoughts
come to me, they are so cold and cheerless; I think you
have come to guard me from evil. I know you are
true and faithful, for my heart says so, and that you will
be my good friend if troubles come."

"I will, Iphi; should trouble come to you I will be
with you, with my very life to offer up in defence. These
nobility people of great families are not with us, nor of us,
nor do they sympathize with us — and their smiles and
favors have oftentimes some sinister meaning or motive,
that we cannot at all times detect."

Iphi's thanks to Jean for his kindness was so full of
love, truth, and sincerity, that his heart was touched with
tenderness for the poor girl, for there was a dread that

some evil was awaiting in the dim, undefined future for
her as well as himself. She was very beautiful, and exposed to the evil designs of others, and he bravely
resolved to do his best to protect her from harm, even
if it involved his life.

He kissed her hand and bid her a cheerful good-by.

Thus these two faithful friends met day after day, until
friendship ripened into the purest love. It was a love that
would have perfumed the shrine of virtue with purity and
innocence. It was with Jean and Iphi like Paul and Annetta.

How the poor and humble sympathize one with the
other. They help each other to carry the burdens and
sorrows of life along its rugged pathways. Their griefs
and cares are not the idle dreams of the imagination, but
stern realities, often realized in absolute want and destitu-
tion. There are in the humble walks of life cares and
sorrows and noble deeds of relief, that the proud, princely
members of the Medici family never dreamed of. In his
leisure hours Jean would call on the good old mother and
father of Iphi, and talk to them of many things appertain-
ing to the cultivation of flowers, vines, &c., also of the
political condition of Italy. The common people of Italy
were not by any means opposed to Napoleon. They com-
prehended the situation of Italy in her political condition,
and rather looked upon Napoleon with favor. He was
regarded as the friend of the people, instead of the nobles.
Austria was of course the lion in the path of perfect re-
concilation.

BOOK IV.

I.

PAUL AND ANNETTA.

A day of joy follows the gloom of night.
As the sun-light follows the fleeing shadow.

WE will leave Leghorn with its pretty Iphi, the flower girl, and its enchanting siren of the Vilani palace and go back, after long years have passed away, to that peaceful valley of the Alps in Provence. The horrors of that night on the battle field of Marengo exist but in memory. Its memories are sorrowful. But, thanks to the heroic dead, they have given a new splendor to the image of Liberty. Man's perfect freedom of mind and body lifts him up on a higher plane of civilization, progress and refinement. All free governments must be for the people.

Every possible encouragement should be given to industry. Peace must also be maintained, and go hand in hand with Liberty. Rigid economy must be the cardinal point with all law-makers, and rulers; so that above all things the burdens of taxation may fall lightly upon the shoulders of honest toil.

Paul Lorraine gradually recovered from the severe wounds he had received at the battle of Marengo. Some time elapsed, however, before he recovered that buoyancy of spirit, robust health, and perfect freedom of action that had marked his boyhood years. He was more quiet and thoughtful, but his generous heart still retained all its kindness to others. The watchful care of his mother,

Annetta, and Louis, very much hastened his recovery to
health. Several years ago Paul had done as he had promised, — come back, and made Annetta his little wife. Truly
this was a union of hands and hearts, and their love was not
of self ; they did not continually plan and act as if their
own individual happiness was the sole, supreme object of
their lives ; it enlarged their affection and made them more
solicitous for the peace and happiness of others. They
fondly caressed that good mother that had so patiently
and fondly prayed and watched over them in the years
of their infancy.

Poor Annetta. Beyond yon sloping hill, that descends
rapidly into the valley, beneath the shadow of the Alpine
cliff and the solemn pines, there is a cemetery, with two
large, newly made graves, and a little one; they are side
by side ; the young and the old repose together.

This cemetery looks so peaceful, so quiet and serene,
with its beautiful green lawn, and sequestered shadows, that
the aching heart might well be tempted to throw away its
pain and anguish, and lay down in peaceful rest. These
were the graves of Annetta's parents, father and mother,
and her first-born, that had passed away in the first year
of its infancy. It was good that Father Gerald had lived
long enough to rejoice over the glad victory of Marengo.
Poor Annetta she was not broken, nor cast down with sorrow, or indulging in vain regrets, yet in her sweet voice
there was a touching, plaintive sadness, when she used to
say to the good mother, or Paul, or Uncle Louis, when
they sought to cheer her in her grief, " No, no : I am not
sad or unhappy. I am not grieving over the loss of dear
ones who have gone before us. I ask how could I be
else than happy, with the love of my dear Paul, mother,

and kind Uncle Louis, and the children here in the valley. No, no, I am not sad ; for surely the good God will permit us to live together again in a far better world than this.

Paul would say : "Annetta, this life here is to me sweet and pleasing. Every object has its inexpressible charms. The forest, the field, the warbling mountain brooks, the grand old hills, the winding road with graceful curves, rising over hills, and falling in the valleys — every object is clothed with hallowed memories of the past, sad and mournful, joyful and happy. Annetta, I love to sit in yonder graveyard where sleep the beloved dead. I love to think of their virtues, and think of our dear little one resting so sweetly in the shadows of the pine and the cliff, and I know full well, Annetta, that its soul, so pure and unstained with the sins of earth, is among the angels of the spirit world. And above all, here dwells our dear mother so precious to us all, and makes us supremely happy while we cheer her in the weary decline of life. I love this place the best of all the earth, for here we learned to love one another. Here we were both born, and here wedded in hand and heart for life."

"Paul," said Annetta, "do you recollect years ago when we selected a star, as a meeting-place for us after death ? It was when we were in our infancy, and yet I recollect it, Paul, as well as if it had been but yesterday."

"Yes, dear Annetta. I have never forgotten it. It was Venus, as evening star, and I have never gazed upon it shining so brightly in the west, over the vine-clad hills, but the image of my beloved is present with me. When in the army in Italy, it blazed with marvellous brilliancy over the towering summit of the Alps, and seemed to tell me that all was peace with the loved ones in this valley ;

and I would say to myself, 'Doubtless Annetta is this moment looking upon this star, and thinking of the absent one.' See, Annetta, it is yonder now, over the western hills in its old place, as we saw it from the cottage of your birth-place, when father and mother Gerald were alive to love and bless their infant children; see, Annetta, how bright it is getting as the shadows of earth arise!"

Annetta's eyes were dimmed with tears, and with a plaintive tone, replied, "Yes, dear Paul; I have often and often looked at that star, and it recalled so vividly the joyful days of our young love; and yet, Paul," —

"Well, Annetta, and yet what? you hesitate."

"Well, dear Paul, oftentimes that star seems to say to me that some great sorrow awaits us all in the years that are coming. I cannot tell why, or what it is, and yet I cannot dispel from my heart this sad foreboding of evil."

"Annetta, it is the sorrows of the past that cast this shadow on your heart, and you mistake it for the shadows of the future. Cheer up, my beloved one; it will be well for us yet; we will see many happy days in this world. I have often wondered what these stars were. There are countless numbers shining and sparkling all over the sky. What do you think they are, Annetta, love?"

There was a flash of inspiration on the sweet, calm face of Annetta, as she answered, " Perhaps they are the beautiful homes of the immortal in heaven. Perhaps God is in the large stars that move across the sky, and guards the good from evil. The falling stars are evil ones who are cast down to earth for their sins. I know God made them, for they are so beautiful and full of promise of a brighter and better world than this. God made all these beautiful things in heaven and earth to cheer us in our weary pilgrimage, and we must love Him, and have faith in Him as our good mother says to us, He will in the end make all things well for us, dear Paul."

Paul looked into the face of Annetta, beaming with love, tenderness and adoration, and his faith in her words was as great as the son of Ancient Israel when he gazed upon the face of the prophet.

She continued, "It is because I love these things so much, and have such faith in God's goodness, that I love my dear Paul so much, and have such an abiding faith in his love for me." She threw her arms around her husband's neck and rested her head upon his bosom.

Let the atheist shatter this vase of faith and love if his heart will allow him.

II.

Prussia Joins the Kings.

Prussia, the powerful and formidable Prussia with her soldiers trained in a school of arms established by Frederick the Great, one of the most remarkable characters that ever figured in history, had declared in favor of Austria and England against the people of France.

It was not vain ambition that prompted Paul Lorraine to again join the army of France.

To him, Napoleon was a majestic figure, heroically standing in defence of justice. He saw that the despotism of the allied powers were seeking to fasten on France the tyranny of the past. He was prompted by patriotism, love of home and country. His sympathies were aroused

by the silent appeals of a bleeding country. The thrilling
words of the Marseillaise, " To arms! To arms," came to
him as the wailing cry of a nation, earnestly pleading for
her sons to fly to her rescue, in the hour of her anguish
and despair.

These solemn pleadings aroused his noble soul, to again
strike for justice, peace, and liberty.

Oftentimes he would say to Annetta, if only France was
at peace, and her people free and prosperous, I could dwell
so happy in this humble home among our dear friends.

Oftentimes, Annetta, Paul, and his mother, would talk
earnestly on this subject ; and their conclusions were
always the same, that the dictates of justice and right
should be followed, and leave the consequence to the
Power above.

Annetta said just as she said to Paul the first time he
was called to the army, " Surely he will come back to
me, for he is good and brave. If he falls, he dies in defence of our dear France, and his memory will be very
dear to me."

That sublime faith in the goodness of the Infinite was
the sheet anchor of the mother. To assist others, make
them happy, and above all things, strictly to perform every
duty required of her in her humble life, was her supreme
happiness.

If the kings, rulers, law-makers, nobility, the wealthy
and powerful of all governments, were controlled in their
actions by such grand and lofty motives as influenced this
humble peasant woman, the husbands, fathers, and sons
would not be dragged off to be sacrificed upon the field of
battle ; and these dear homes, so full of peace, joy, and
happiness, transformed into homes of mournful sadness.

Paul Lorraine, influenced by these motives, and the kind, generous acts of Napoleon in furnishing means to have him removed to his home when wounded at Marengo, could no longer endure the reflection that his heroic countrymen were struggling to defend the liberties of France, while he rested idly, refusing to help in the time of danger and peril. This movement of Prussia at the time, had an ominous look, and Paul is again a soldier in the grand army of France.

BOOK V.

JENA.

Napoleon while defending France,
The crowned heads charge him with ambition.

PRUSSIA is now in the arena of war, to meet France in the contest of arms.

Frederick the Great, during his lifetime, had raised Prussia up to the position of one of the most opulent and powerful nations in Europe. Under his direction and superintendence, the army of Prussia advanced to a position of military skill and discipline, that was not surpassed, if equalled, by the army of any other nation. There was some decline in this condition of things during the reign of his nephew, but William III, had again restored prosperity and power in Prussia.

This was the army that Napoleon had to encounter, on the field of Jena, in 1806. Jena could not be called a battle; it was a duel between two gladiators of equal strength, skill, and courage. The Prussian says, "You shall perish on this battle-field." The Frenchman says, "I come, resolved on victory or death! Strike!" This condition of things made it an encounter of life or death, between two of the grandest armies in Europe; made it one of the most terrible battle-fields in loss of life, comparing the numbers engaged on each side, recorded in history.

It was the grim banquet of death, the goblets overflowed with the red current of life. The carnival was brilliant with the flames of war. The music was the cannon's roar, the clash of arms, and the cry of "Charge, brave men, charge!" Now the valiant Prussian is pressing down the grand banners of France. Then comes, as if from some dark abyss, a charge that strikes dismay to the Prussian. Is this victory? No! The Prussian, like some wonderful athlete in the game of death, recovers from the shock and is eager for the contest. The victory is poised over the bloody field. Truly this was Greek confronting Greek. Reserved troops had been marched into battle to fill up the depleted ranks on both sides.

The man on horseback on the summit of Landgraphenberg was looking thoughtfully and serenely upon the battle-field. Yet his fate is in the balance. Surely he must be prescient. That mighty brain is calculating chances. Nothing escapes his eagle glance. He is surrounded with the Imperial Guards.

It is Jove on Mount Olympus. The Imperial Guard is the thunderbolt, poised in his grasp, ready to strike when the auspicious moment comes.

The Guard was mounted, and in order. At their head was a man mounted on a black horse.

He is clothed in sable garments, with a white plume. It is Murat. His face is pale, cold, and passionless. He looks the classic personification of Mars, wrought from marble by the skillful hand of supreme art. Cold as he appeared to be in this moment of extreme peril, there was in his breast a volcano of wrath. He saw the sons of France fall in battle, and his brave heart and strong arm were not there to strike and save. The Austrian said of him, "He is the fiend of war." The Frenchman said, "No, he is the angel of mercy." Who would suppose that

cold face, so stern, so rigid in battle, had a heart often
moved to tears of pity and compassion, a heart that was
truly merciful. He said, " Never, never have I looked
upon a man, and then killed him. His image would have
embittered my existence."

The order came at last to General Murat to charge.
Like the mighty mountain torrent, down rushed the column
of armed heroes, sweeping on bravely to the contest. The
rising and falling of the hill and plain, in their undula-
tions, gave it the appearance of a vast serpent, with the
fleetness of the wind. There was a blow, a crash. The
Prussians received the charge with courage, but it was too
much for mortal man to endure. Wherever that dark figure with the white plume went, the guard followed. The
enemy disappeared as if confronted by the angels of death.
It is no longer a battle, but a carnage. Although the
Prussian army was driven, and absolutely forced from the
field, never, perhaps, in the world's history were they surpassed in the skill, courage, and true heroism they displayed on the battle field of Jena.

Napoleon's victory at Jena was a decree against the
crowned heads of Europe interfering with the divine right
of the people of France, in their glorious struggle to establish self-government. Soon, and he was in possession of
the city of Berlin, and the tomb of Frederick the Great.
He accepted the surrender of the one, and with reverence
stood in the presence of the other. It was the supreme
majesty of life ; standing with reverential awe in the solemn shadows of the tomb of the majestic dead.

This victory made Napoleon the master of the situation.
The king of Spain surrendered ; he placed his brother
Joseph on the throne. Joseph, having resigned the posi-

tion of king of Naples, Joachim Murat, the husband of
Caroline Bonaparte, was placed on this vacant throne with
the title of king of Naples.

We have gone aside out of our pathway in speaking of
this battle of Jena, for the reason that, if Napoleon had
lost the battle of Jena, there would have been no occasion
to have written anything about the life of Paul Lorraine.
He was with Jean Gendron on that fearful battle-field,
fighting with true heroism in defence of France. Strange
it was that, at this battle Paul was unharmed, and without
a single wound, while Jean was severely wounded. Paul
had now the chance to repay in part Jean's kindness at
Marengo, where he saved his life. Jean soon recovered
from his injury, and he and Paul being in the same regiment, were in the battles of Eylau and Friedland, and
when the army of Napoleon moved south, they both, with
the third regiment, went into garrison at Leghorn, and remained there until Joachim Murat was placed in the position of king of Naples.

BOOK VI.

VILANI PALACE.

I.

A MERCIFUL KING.

LIBERTY won a victory at Jena, yet the memory of the conflict is full of mournful pathos. Murat is now king of Naples. He is the noble king of the people — not the despotic king of the nobles. It was joy to his heart to see a stately ship sail into the bay of Naples, bearing aloft the proud ensign of the stars and stripes of the glad Republicans across the sea. Right joyful would it be for such generous souls, if the glad songs of liberty could be sung to sympathizing hearts in every land. That the sunshine of peace would drive away from every nation, from every household, the dismal shadows of relentless war, and kings, presidents, law-makers, and rulers, deal honestly and justly with the people.

Paul Lorraine and his good friend Jean, are at Leghorn, as their regiments were being garrisoned at that place, with Col. Count Vilani as commander of the garrison. His headquarters were established there. Iphi is still the happy flower-girl we left at Leghorn a few years ago, acting as the good angel to the declining years of her aged parents. A little sad, perhaps, owing to the absence of her Jean, as she called him, but his return had brought to her face the smile of joy. This girl in the lowest walks of life, had learned a grand philosophy in human happiness, that is not taught in the female seminary, or in the college, or any institution of learning. It did not come to her through the study of ancient lore, the study of the dead languages, the splendid songs of the poet, the eloquence of the orator, or the brilliant pages of history wrought out by the genius of the historian. Her innocent, untutored heart said to her, "Iphi, the only true foundation for happiness to us mortals, is by making others happy." Virtue says crown all with smiles — vice, curse all with tears. She still went to the palace of Vilani with flowers and fruits, where she met the siren smile of Verono, the lustful gaze of Count Vilani and the hard features of Geno. There were times when this grand palace and its inmates would cast a chilling shadow on her young heart, but she was happy, her parents were contented. Jean had come back well, and full of joy, and she never dreamed that any one would do her harm, or make her the victim of base schemes and sinful purposes. Sad is it to think that innocence and virtue, relying on the truth and sincerity of others, are so easily betrayed.

Verono was the reverse of Iphi; her secret hate for the humble flower-girl was intense. Were Iphi upon the altar of sacrifice, to appease an offended goddess, she would have brought no offering to save. The tears of innocence and beauty would but aggravate her passion of hate and malice. She would save if the act would be instrumental in the advancement of her lust for power and the unholy flame of ambition, that had consumed every virtue and every generous feeling of her heart.

Verono was Iphi reversed. The vase of life and joy

was reversed into an urn of death and sorrow. The poison concealed in the head of the serpent, with its shining diamond eyes, so skilfully wrought on the ring on her finger was no more deadly to human life, than the poison in her heart was deadly to human happiness. Silently and fatally, the serpent was charming the nightingale, so full of sweet song, to destruction.

Verono, wrapt in her dark and terrible thoughts, was seated in one of the most gorgeous apartments of the Vilani palace, surrounded by every luxury and splendor that wealth and art could procure. She was in the presence of Da Vinci's portraits of her ancestors, taken from life. One of them was a female form, young in years, that glowed with angelic beauty. Surely those eyes are alive with the grand thoughts of a living brain. Surely those lips will utter gentle words of love and affection. Were you to gaze upon that picture, long would your heart wish to linger and dwell in the presence of its exalted inspiration. When you turn and leave it, that image with eyes and lips so full of truth, sincerity and love, would ever cling to your memory.

Yet all this did not move Verono from weaving some dark scheme, that her fertile brain had wrought out, to gratify her heart's deadly lust of power and ambition. She uttered these ominous words: "There are too many witnesses to the accursed secrets of my life. Count Vilani is in love, yes, in love in his way, with that pretty, simple face of the flower-girl. I will use the one to destroy and blast the other. That wolf Geno, I will drag into the meshes of the net, and cast him into the pit. Then there is left Alonzo. Ha, ha, ha, right easily can I control the simple Alonzo, and control him to my liking. Then shall

I be the grand triumphant mistress of this palace, and that hidden wealth, concealed away in secret places, and covered with the dark pall of crime. Why is it that my soul loves to dwell in these gloomy shadows? It is because they suggest to me vengeance, power, and gratified ambition. I will be but avenging my wrongs. Vilani betrayed me; led me from virtue into crime. Now, to me, there is enchantment in the gloomy realms of iniquity. Doubtless the evil spirit that turned the happiness of Eden into anguish and woe, had fiendish delight in its work of ruin, and longed for more victims to drink from the poisoned cup. I must have victims to appease the cruel demon enshrined in my soul. Henceforward, there is nothing left for me but ambition, proud, lofty ambition, to rule and to ruin.

"These plans may leave myself and Alonzo alone: I the mistress, he the slave. Should he dare to disobey me, or spurn my least commands, how easily that little talisman [looking at the ring] could forever silence the last witness of my shame and crime. Its slightest sting is death. It is said by some wise ones, that my ancestors used such instruments to open the pathway for the triumph of ambition. If so, why not I?"

Alonzo enters with a meek and suppliant air, and says—

"I hope I am not intruding on the privacy of my lady, or disturbing her meditations. If so, I ask pardon."

"Pardon is surely granted my best friend. Really there is no intrusion. I was this moment thinking of summoning you to my presence, Alonzo. I have some thoughts to suggest; you are surely most welcome."

"Do you know that I was right in my conjectures," she continued, "that Vilani had fallen in love with the pretty face of this simple flower girl? ha, ha, ha! How ridiculous! how absurd! But Alonzo, this dull, monotonous life we are now leading, with that dread mystery hanging like a cloud over us, with Vilani's licentious smile, and Geno's villainous looks makes life here in this palace dull, insipid, and tasteless. I have resolved to gratify his passion after his style, or rather Vilani's plan of dethroning virtue — with the mockery of the sanctity of marriage. You have made for him an excellent priest on several occasions, and I propose to have you try your skill by uniting the nobleman with the peasant girl, Iphi. Alonzo, I have a keen relish for this interesting performance, for well you know that I was myself a victim : and it would please me so much to see others fall before this hypocritical monster; ha, ha, ha! It makes you tremble; surely my Alonzo is not a coward?"

"Pardon me, Lady Verono. I was thinking that this might lead to the disclosure of secrets, that we might all wish to conceal."

"All folly, man; there is nothing to conceal. What do I care for the cowardly, craven gossips of Leghorn, or all Italy. I could fell them with frowns. I tell you this leads to power and wealth. Listen, — do my bidding. All you are required to do is to say nothing — look and act by instructions. You may have to put on priestly robes; take the holy book, mumble some blessings and prayers; just as you have often done before to please Vilani, and this will also be to him a pleasing service."

"Lady Verono, I fear — yet I must obey your commands to the letter. Instruct me when the time comes, and I am your humble, obedient servant and friend."

"Good Alonzo, I know that to do my bidding is to thee

a pleasure, and I shall be sure and quick in rewarding you
for your friendship and kindness. I will see to it that you
have proper instructions to perform your part, so that this
drama will result to our liking and gain. You know that
while this palace is hereditary in this family, yet to a very
great extent you and I are mere tenants. It matters not
now that I should tell you my plans, for I must look well
to the events that may arise in the progress of things, and
if my good Alonzo has perfect faith in my tact, skill and
daring, he will follow and obey orders." Alonzo expressed
himself as having his fate in the hands of Verono. He was
well aware that he dare not deny this proud, cruel, and
talented woman perfect supremacy over him in all things.
He knew full well that in that wonderful brain and heart
there was a will and ambition that would hesitate at nothing to accomplish a purpose. He knew from the experience of former days, when terrible acts were committed,
that he dare not even argue the feasibility of her schemes,
that she had adopted with regard to Vilani and Iphi, and
that to interfere with any suggestion or objection would be
to hazard his own existence.

II.

COUNT VILANI.

COLONEL VILANI had his headquarters in the garrison
under his control and command. In this garrison was the
regiment to which Paul Lorraine and Jean Gendron were
attached. It is known to many persons that the soldiers
in the ranks always form a correct conclusion of the

character of their commander, or the peculiar traits of
character of each prominent officer. Col. Vilani was
very despotic and unreasonable in many of his rules and
orders. He was also of that temperament that he could
not conceal his prejudices. Pride and vanity were exceedingly prominent. He was continually guilty of little,
petty acts of tyranny towards this regiment to which Paul
Lorraine was attached, on account of its complete French
character. When he had the appointing of subordinates,
he selected men of the same cast of character as himself,
and generally Italians. He was cunning enough, however,
not to commit any overt act, upon which could be based a
charge with any possibility of maintaining it. In fact, his
peculiar friends and associates would swear him out of
any difficulty whatever. Thus it was that there was a
silent, growing hatred in the regiment for Vilani. Paul
Lorraine had been raised to the position of second lieutenant, and had been always prompt to allay any feeling
against him, for fear that it would break out into open rup-
ture. Louis Dejon had been drafted into one of the regiments in the garrison that was stationed in the immediate
control of the officers at headquarters, and had been, on
account of his friendship for Iphi and her parents, a
good, sincere friend of Jean's, and also of Paul Lorraine's.
Although Louis was an Italian, these three young men
became very sincere friends and companions, and doubtless would stand by one another in any emergency or
danger. Oftentimes they would relate to one another the
events of their lives, and those connected with them, so
that there soon was formed a bond of union and affection
that added much to their individual happiness and contentment in the dull hours of garrison life.

Time moved along; the Lady Verono still bestowed upon the flower girl her smiles and patronage, and Iphi's life was still tranquil in the performance of affection and duty. Verono seemed now at times more inquisitive, and her searching questions would at times startle Iphi, as having some sinister motive in this curiosity.

She said to her on one occasion, "Iphi, you have a good friend besides your parents. Have you not?"

"Oh, yes, lady, there is Louis Dejon, who is to us a good friend, and has been so for many years! He has labored for us in the garden, and is a good hand at flowers and vegetables. He is now in the army and in the garrison."

"Have you not others?"

"Oh, yes: there is Jean Gendron, who is my best friend, and he is so very good, and noble, my lady, and I love Jean very much."

"Then Iphi, I see this Jean is your sweetheart, and you are lovers. Well, is this all your friends? And Jean is a soldier, I suppose?"

"Yes, my lady. and these two — Louis and Jean, have formed a friendship with a noble-looking French soldier, whose name is Paul Lorraine, who is a good friend to us all."

"Paul Lorraine! The name indicates good lineage, and he is a soldier. Well, Iphi, you have an army at your back — so many gallant soldiers — and one of them a lover."

"Yes, my lady, but I put no reliance on that. I do not like the necessity that calls so many good young men in the army to be killed. It were far better they were employed in some useful industry, than wasting their time in camps, marches, battle fields and garrisons. I treat every one kindly and justly, and every one seems to be my friend. I do not know any one who would harm or injure me. I know not of even one that I have cause to fear."

"Iphi," replied Verono, "you are but little versed in this world's ways — its passions and its ambitions."

Thus the time passed, until one day Verono invited Iphi up into one of the fine apartments in the palace, and she was highly pleased with the works of art, and the splendid furniture and embellishment that surrounded her. The most humble Italian peasants have excellent taste, and a just appreciation of the beautiful in art. They inherit this fine taste from their ancestors. If an Italian buys a piece of sculpture or painting, or builds a house, or fits up apartments or rooms, he evinces excellent taste, and his judgment in such matters is artistic.

Verono says to Iphi, "Would you not like to reside in this fine mansion, among these beautiful things, ride in a carriage, have your servants, and live like a grand lady in fine style, and have plenty of money, and buy your parents a nice farm and home. I ask you this, for Vilani is willing to make you his wife. He loves you dearly, for you are so beautiful. Then you will be mistress of all this house and servants, and every one will obey your commands."

"Oh, my lady, you are but jesting, or it is perhaps a piece of mirthfulness on your part; or is it a mockery of my humble condition?"

She gazed intently into the face of lady Verono, and saw to her dismay that her words had a terrible meaning. For the first time her trembling heart was shadowed with the dark spirit of evil, vaguely outlined to her sight, but none the less terrible.

The beautiful form of the Lady Verono, that she loved so well, seemed to pass from her, and left her in the presence of a stern, relentless fiend. For a a moment she thought she was in a horrible dream, and the terrible abyss that was yawning in her pathway was but the delusion of a feverish brain. In a moment she regained her senses, and saw her terrible situation.

Lady Verono changed her tone to one of tenderness and compassion and then said :

" Iphi, hear me. This is the proposal of Vilani. Be composed, and do not be so startled and terrified ; gather your senses about you and act calmly."

" I will, my lady, and I will answer your question calmly and sincerely. You asked me if I would not like to live in this palace, have carriages to ride in, and servants, and be the mistress of all this wealth and elegance. I say no, my lady — I was born among the poor, raised among the humble ; and, like Jesus, ' I love the poor.' He said the humility of this earth should be exalted in heaven. And when he said, ' suffer little children,' he called the child of the cottage as well as the child of the palace. The Infinite said, through the holy One who died on the cross, ' love one another.' Lady, the splendors of earth beget pride, envy and ambition. The humble cot where lives those dear ones of my heart, is to me the dearest spot on all this earth. I would not cast from me the happiness of parental love, were you to give me in exchange a crown, sceptre, or kingdon. My parents are happy because their wants are few, and what little they have of this world's goods they share with those in need. And my lady, if you only knew how grateful they felt for your kindness to me, and how they have prayed so fervently for your happiness, you surely would love them. There is my dear Jean, I would not cast him from me for all the grand things you could do for me in this world. He is so good, true, and noble. It would break his heart ; and you yourself, dear lady, would pity his grief and sorrow. Were you to witness the agony of my poor old father and mother, were I to desert them for a life of splendid dishonor, it would move you to tears. The song of the bird is sad, imprisoned even in a cage of gold. The lamb at nightfall seeks the parental fold, and the young bird the nest where loving wings are spread for its protection — so would I away to you humble cot, to bask in the love of those good hearts, who have watched with tender care over me all the years of my life. Oh, my lady, it cannot be, it cannot be."

Lady Verono, unmoved by the tears and the pathetic appeals of Iphi, says, " Why, simpleton, can it be possible that any one in this world is so void of ambition ? The story of the cross is a myth ; Jesus, lover of mankind, a delusion. This woeful tale of crucifixion will pass away, like the Egyptian worship of Isis and the Grecian worship of Jupiter, into the shadows of the past, and vanish like the brilliant conceptions of poetic dreams. Why, you would drag the church, with all its grandeur and magnificence, its pride and ambition, down to a level with Bethlehem — its manger, its outcast people, driven from the splendor of Jerusalem. What folly ! Money, gold, will cure the wounded hearts of the parents As to this foolish love of your Jean, the world scorns the paltry sentiment. Let your Jean march off to the battle-field ; you be proud and ambitious. It is your fate. Accept it and be content."

"My lady, these cruel words you have spoken are terrible. These vain, idle worships of antiquity, I know not of, nor do I care for them. Jerusalem, with all its splendor, was destroyed through its vanity and ambition. Yet, Jesus sorrowed for it, with all its crimes and misfortunes. The religion of Jesus has an imperishable grandeur: it is love for all mankind, and will be with him forever; follow him in all his wanderings in life, heal his wounds, cure his anguish, and dry his tears. It cannot perish, until every noble impulse, every grand emotion of love, truth, and mercy shall perish in the human heart. You ask me to forsake my parents and my dear Jean. When my heart ceases to love them with a holy, tender love, it will cease to throb in this world. Sooner would I die than to say I have ceased to love them and they are no longer dear to me." Iphi could see no consolation in the stern, unfeeling look of Verono. This woman, whom she had all the time loved so well for her kindness, was now to her terrible and appalling. "Then you have no pity for me. You cannot say to me, with kindness and compassion, 'Go, Iphi, go and seek happiness in thine own way?'"

"No, foolish girl, all I can say is, it is your fate; accept it and be content;" and she left the apartment.

Poor Iphi! the dark abyss was before her; how terrible, that this pure and lofty soul should be the victim of such cruelty and wrong! She clasped her hands together, and in the deepest tones of agony and despair, exclaimed, "O God, I am lost, I am lost. My poor father, my poor mother, and my Jean. Oh, how their hearts will bleed for me." She could stand no longer, and sank tremblingly upon a seat with her face buried in her hands, until a flood of tears for a time soothed the aching heart.

These two human souls had come to earth in the same Christian land, the same fold, the same church and creed, yet how widely different in thought, character, and action. Iphi, like the wise men of the East, when the star of Bethlehem led them to the infant laid in the manger, and appearing thus in lowly life, were not dismayed or disheartened, but worshipped him as the holy one, and said, "The splendors of earth are nothing in the balance against the glory of the Infinite."

She had received in her young heart all that fine inspiration that comes from great virtue connected with perfect humility, so prominent in the life of Jesus. She loved his name, for it was full of the glad memories of acts of charity and mercy. His life among the lowly, the poor, and the outcast, came to her view clothed with ineffable grandeur.

She practiced to others, charity, kindness and mercy ; and the happiness she brought to them, filled her life with perfect joy. She was ever the good Samaritan, to turn from her pathway to heal the wounds of the dying stranger.

Lady Verono was the reverse of all this. She could not conceive how any one could be enraptured over a life of humility. This wonderful feeling of love for Jesus and parental affection, manifested in the action of Iphi, was to her mind the very extreme of folly. She looked upon this story of the Cross just as the Egyptian looked upon the story of Isis and her lost Osiris, or the Greek upon his Jupiter, enthroned in grandeur on Mount Olympus.

She did not accuse the church with misrepresenting the teachings of Jesus, for she admired the church for its pride, power, splendor, and ambition.

She would have justified the archbishop of Pisa, in removing by assassination the Medici, even to give place to the Pazzi ; if this act resulted in addition of power and splendor to the church. She would, of course, justify Catherine de Medicis of France in all her acts of ghastly cruelty, if she realized the lofty aims of her towering ambition. She would have passed on the other side, where lay the wounded and dying stranger, for she knew no prompting of pity or compassion.

Verono's great talents, wealth, and high social position, made her life brilliant, and drew the admiration of mankind.

Iphi had none of these things to offer. She was poor, humble and content. All she had to offer to this world's homage and praise was a grand soul, formed and fashioned in the image of God.

BOOK VII.

I.

IPHI BETRAYED.

The Shepherd goes to the wolf,
To seek the lamb that is lost.

THE parents of Iphi were much alarmed at her absence. They watched for her through the twilight and the midnight hour; the dawn of day came and passed away with the bright morn shining on land and sea, yet she came not. This was sorrowful. Surely some calamity had befallen this child, the prop of old age, the joyful light.

There was to them a strange, fearful foreboding of evil.

Year after year, Iphi had returned to her home as sure as the night follows the day. They could make no possible conjecture of what had happened her. She had no enemies. It was not possible that this innocent child could be the object of any criminal purpose, that there was any one so base and cruel as to wrong or injure their darling child. They knew nothing of the perils of a world they had seen but little of. The first suggestion that came to their minds, was to send to the palace to see if anything could be learned as to her absence.

One of the kind, sympathizing neighbors volunteered to look up Louis and Jean, and also to go to the palace and make inquiry of the whereabouts of the lost Iphi. He returned, bringing both Louis and Jean with him. He had also been to the palace, and came with the report from

the servant that she had been there, but had departed
at about the usual hour.

Jean and Louis urged the father and mother not to despair. They firmly believed that she would be found
unharmed, and that nothing would be left undone to find
her out and rescue her. They both felt anxious to see
Paul Lorraine, to consult with him, and advise about the
best way to act in this sorrowful affair. Poor Jean concealed his agony and tears. His alarm was far greater
than any one could discover by his outward action. He
had within him a dreadful, vague impression that the villainy of Colonel Count Vilani was in some way the cause
of Iphi's abduction, and when he, Paul, and Louis got
together and talked over the matter, Louis said that several times when Colonel Vilani had his carousals, he over-
heard his contemptible vain boast of the number of his
conquests in the court of love.

Paul saw with dismay, that there was, alas, to much truth
in the conclusions of Jean and Louis, that poor Iphi was
in the power of Vilani. He was the commander of the
garrison, prominent among the nobility, wealthy and influ-
ential. The whole entire police force in the most of the
Italian States, are the willing tools of the nobility. Surely
so when there is money to bribe and corrupt. Paul saw
that no charge could be made to any authority, with the
mere surmise that he was the man who was at the bottom
of this villainy.

If Paul had any evidence whatever, he would have
applied to the king of Naples for redress.

But there was nothing upon which to base a charge.
He therefore resolved to save her at the peril of his life.
He thought of his own dear Annetta so far away from him,

yet she seemed to be present urging him to rescue Iphi.

Paul saw that some plan must be adopted to enter the palace, and find out if the poor girl was in fact kept imprisoned there against her will, and if so, he would take enough force with him, to rescue her at all hazards, and depend on the justice of the cause.

He thought of Louis: he knew that Louis was acquainted with Geno, and believed he could manage Geno, so that he would divulge something that would lead to the knowledge they desired.

II.

LOUIS DEJON.

Louis was not long in throwing himself in the way of Geno.

"Well, comrade," says Geno, upon meeting Louis, "what's the word, good or bad?"

"Bad, faithful Geno, very bad; I am suffering with poverty, poverty! I see others enjoying themselves, while I, poor soul, have not wherewith to buy a glass of wine. If I had some gold, I would know how to spend it, and live a jolly life."

"Louis, I have ever looked upon thee as an honest knave, and true to a comrade. Wilt swear by the holy cross to divide, truly and faithfully, with an honest friend?"

"I will swear Geno, to divide all the gold I get by thy council and direction; does that suffice?"

"It is enough, Louis."

"Then by my holy faith I am your man, but listen,

if you betray me, my dagger seeks your heart : remember this, my motto, ' dead men are silent.' "

These words, spoken so firm, with that look of deep resolve, made the cowardly heart of Geno tremble.

"Never fear me, good Louis, we are of the same kind, and comrades, and must needs stand together."

" Now then, Louis, to the gold. A comrade in the palace, a servant of Vilani, his name Joseph, he and myself, have at different times found gold in unsafe places in the palace. We have gathered it and divided it into two sacks, marking the sacks in this way. My sack is fastened with twine, his with a wire ; they are concealed in a waste-room, on the northeast angle, on the third floor of the palace, in a closet, at the bottom, under some rubbish."

" Well, Geno, what is to hinder you from taking the gold yourself."

" I will tell you Louis why. Joseph and myself are on the watch and guard together. Before we go on duty, Joseph examines the concealed treasure by himself ; we will be together in the morning and examine. The gold is gone. I say Joseph you have robbed me. When you came alone to examine on last evening you done it. I threaten his life, he is terrified, and trembles, pleads for mercy, and promises to soon steal enough to make good my loss. I am convinced he is honest, and say poor Joseph, I forgive you this time, now see to it that you pay me. Thus you see, I put him in the place of the wrong doer, and I honest Geno, the sufferer. Now this is my offer: I will give you the key of the postern gate that leads to a secret passage, landing on the third floor of the palace, through a sliding panel at the head of the stairway. On the inside of the postern gate you will find a dark lantern, with match, etc. You will bring with you both sacks, and conceal them in some safe place, until to-morrow, when I will see you, and divide with you Joseph's sack of gold. Is it a bargain?"

"It is a bargain, honest Geno, and I accept and swear; but now tell me, why this watch and guard duty of yours and Joseph's?"

"That, Louis, does not concern the gold; that is a private affair of the count's, and you must not descend to the second floor, or you will surely be discovered, and get into trouble."

"But, good Geno, what is this little private affair of the count's; surely you can trust a friend, and tell him this much, when it is of little importance."

"Well, it is a love affair of the count's, and you surely can get no pay out of such trifles as that; get the gold, and let the count and the lady go to the devil. Let the count fall in love, and we will see to his gold."

"Is that all, good Geno? and then I will surely not disturb the noble count in his love matters."

Thus it was, that Louis in his blank face and fine talk, had obtained from Geno, the cunning rogue, all he desired. When Geno left him, Louis said to himself, "what a villian he is; he even robs a partner. I must now see Paul and Jean, and arrange our plans."

After consulting with them, it was agreed that at midnight, Louis should enter the palace, and discern, if possible, the exact position of things, and then to act upon his information, and to be prepared at any moment to enter the palace, through this passage, and rescue Iphi by main force if necessary."

Accordingly, at the midnight hour, he entered the postern gate, and found the lantern, and then proceeded to the secret entrance, mounted the stairway with the aid of his lantern, and came to the sliding panel. Here he took the precaution to darken his light, and then with the utmost caution he moved back the panel, and stood in what seemed to him a passage, having at the far end from where he stood a large window, covered with a curtain, through which the light was dimly shining. He stopped and listened, and he certainly heard voices, in conversation, but could catch no words spoken. Soon, two dark figures moved across the disk of the window, and they appeared to be approaching the place where he stood. At length he caught the name of Paul Lorraine quite distinctly.

He at once concluded that it had some reference to Iphi. Yet he could not hear enough to make any connection in the conversation, they being some distance from him, but evidently coming near.

He reflected a moment, and thought his best course was to lie prostrate, close to the wall of the passage, and far enough from any side entrance, in case they should pass out.

Soon they came quite close to where he lay concealed by darkness. He heard the words, "Alonzo, do not rest secure in your position in the palace, on account of any generosity on the part of Vilani, for he is base, cruel, and heartless. That peasant-girl in his power, he would despoil her of virtue, then command Geno to assassinate her, and conceal his crime. He will soon be bringing to the palace a wife from nobility of a century's growth, and compel you and I to take positions of servitude, base menials, to await the pleasure of the Count and Countess Vilani."

"You know Alonzo that in case of his death I am the sole heir of the name and fortune of the house of Vilani —and the offspring of a legitimate marriage, would forever debar me from the inheritance."

"Why not you, my lady, wed Vilani, and become the countess, and all will then end well."

"I did, in the days of my innocence, wed him in good faith; but you know the horrid mockery on his part, and the cruel betrayal."

"Oh, my lady you have forgiven me for the part I took in that accursed crime; for I was driven by desperation to commit the deed, and thought it best, to save you from a worse fate. Forgive him, he is anxious; and has often expressed a desire to unite the only two living lineal descendants of the house of Vilani, in marriage."

"Wed him, Alonzo? I would just as soon wed the serpent; his very look is loathing, his very touch is contamination. Wed Count Vilani? I would far sooner send him after the murdered Francisco, and cast his body in the vaults beneath this palace. He would in order to pander to his lust, or his ambition, go before the Tribunal and charge us with the murder of Francisco; procure false witnesses, bribe the police and the courts, and have us both put to death, for a crime committed by his own orders and commands. Yes Alonzo, sooner than again submit to his loathing embrace, the fatal talisman shall do its evil work."

"Oh, my lady that is cruel; pardon, pardon and forgive him; but when is this mockery of marriage to be consumated?"

"To-morrow night, when the cathedral clock strikes the midnight hour, and you Alonzo, are commanded to perform the act of profanation."

Louis thus received more intelligence than he supposed was possible. He was horrified with Lady Verono's statement of the crimes perpetrated in this house. Her description of the infamous Vilani was terrible. Iphi was in great danger. He saw that she must be rescued from her situation and that no time was to be lost.

Lady Verono and Alonzo moved back towards the window, and were out of distinct hearing; but soon returned, with the apparent intention of separating. They were not now moving as close together as when first they came in range of the window light. He heard Alonzo ask some question as to Iphi and the marriage ceremony, to be performed between her and Count Vilani, and caught these words distinctly from Lady Verono's lips:

"To-morrow night when the cathedral clock strikes the hour of twelve — "

For some time Louis lay rapt in thought. He was perplexed. Should he retire and bring back with him Paul and Jean? or should he wait until the hour of twelve to-morrow night, and come prepared to carry Iphi away from this accursed den of guilt and infamy, at all hazards?

The question of the money, and returning the key to Geno on the morrow, perplexed him. If he left the money Geno would conclude he had betrayed him, and might think and act so that it would interfere with his plans in retaining the key to the gate, as well as the secret entrance into the palace.

He waited for some time, until he thought everything was quiet. He had heard the retreating footsteps of

Verono in one direction and Alonzo in the other. Then
he walked along close to the wall until he approached the
door leading into the room described by Geno. The door
was unlocked, and he stood inside of the room, and
for a moment listened to catch any sound. It was as
silent as a tomb. Light struggled into the apartment
through the partly closed shutters; he could see no objects
in the room distinctly. He closed the door behind him
opened his dark lantern, and passed its light slowly around
the room. It was as Geno had said, a rubbish or waste
room. It had a dismal and dreary appearance. Among
the old rubbish of the apartment there were some cast-
aside paintings, among which Louis discovered the por-
trait of a strange face, taken in boyhood. On the back
of the canvass was written the name of Francisco Vilani.
This, then, was the name connected with crime, spoken of
by Verono but a few moments since; when all at once the
dark story of the life of Count Vilani, and his insane
cousin came to his mind. "Ah! this is where this gold
comes from that keeps this palace shining in such splendor. The very gold that I have taken upon myself to
carry away is part of the fruit of this accursed crime."

He went to the closet, and there beneath the rubbish
lay the two bags of gold. The mouth of one sack was
closed with some thin wire, the other with twine-string.

What next? He seated himself and thought of his
next course. Will he go below and grope around, and
find the place where Iphi was imprisoned, go after Jean
and Paul and rescue her? In case he should be discovered, he would ruin all. He felt sure now that no violence
would be offered Iphi, until the hour of that mockery of
marriage that Verono spoke of — when the cathedral

clock strikes the hour of midnight. He also concluded to take the gold with him, and convince Geno, that his designs were not to interfere with anything further in the palace, and he would make some plausible excuse for retaining the keys of the gate and secret entrance into the palace. With these conclusions he took the two sacks of gold and was about to depart on his way through the panel in the wall, the secret stairway, and out of the gate. But on turning around the light of his lamp fell upon the dark form of Alonzo, gazing upon him in perfect amazement. Louis instantly grasped his stiletto, not to make an attack on Alonzo, but to defend his life at all hazards.

Put up thy weapon, rash man. You are in my power. In one moment of time I can arouse assistance, and you will be beyond all earthly power. I have fixed the sliding panel, so that were you to attempt to open it, you would spring an alarm that would insure your destruction. I have discovered you in the commission of a crime that the laws of the land punish with death.

Noble Louis came to rescue Iphi from the grasp of the monster, and will himself fall a sacrifice to his merciless vengeance. He came to save, and is cruelly lost.

When Alonzo left Verono in the passage she went in the same direction that Louis had to go to reach the waste chamber, where this gold was concealed. Alonzo took the other end of the passage that led to another angle of the palace. Alonzo heard, or thought he heard, some person moving on the floor, and chanced to turn and look back just at the moment Louis raised himself up in an upright position and passed between him and the dimly lighted disk of the same window where Louis had first seen the dimly-defined forms of Alonzo and Verono, approaching the place where he lay concealed against the wall.

Alonzo glided, softly back heard Louis open the door and close it after him ; saw the flash of the lantern as it passed the door, and when Louis stooped down and took the two sacks of gold out of the closet he saw him plainly, as the closet was in the opposite side of the room and nearly in a direct line. He gently opened the door and stepped into the room. The noise drew the attention of Louis. He raised himself up, turned the light in that direction, and there stood Alonzo looking at him in the very act of robbery.

III.

THE SIREN AND VICTIM.

WE left Iphi in the power of Verono, left her in despair, with a heart suffering the pangs of sorrow. It was not for self she grieved, but those blessed ones in yonder cottage, upon whom this blow would fall with crushing force. Surely their hearts will break with the loss of their Iphi. Verono had returned to her, and, with that mysterious transformation of tone and manner, was addressing with apparent affection, her helpless victim.

" Iphi," she says, "your cottage, your flower-garden, and vineyard, you love so well, will soon look to you as unimportant and contemptible. Your petty dreams of happiness, and contentment are vain and childish fancies. In the course of nature your father and mother, must soon pass away, and leave you alone in the world. What you call virtue, will soon be to you a fanciful image, clothed with the roseate hues of a youthful, joyous imagination, but empty, shining bubbles, that disappear with the world's rude touch. Your dear Jean, as you call him, will either fall in battle or be cast away as a mere waif, floating on the world's wide sea. You thought me charming and delightful, and yet I am but a sample of the world's deceit and ambition. The world awards a premium to successful ambition, while it uses virtue and credulity as instruments to accomplish its purposes and designs. To-day those you love seem happy and joyous, to-morrow they are tossed helplessly upon the waves, with none to help, save, or pity. Soon, very soon you, with your beautiful face and fine form, will fall a victim to some one's passion and treachery. Act for yourself. Here is a palace and wealth, and fine apparel for you to wear. You will be a lady. Gold is our best friend. Cast away these idle fancies of youth, called morality and virtue. Face the world with courage, pride, and ambition."

To Iphi these words, though uttered in a friendly tone and with apparent sincerity, were strange and dreadful. Her heart was so stricken that it almost ceased to throb. Her love for her parents, her Jean, as she called him, her charity for every one, was as true and sublime as that charity that said to the thief dying on the cross, with all his crimes upon him, "This day thou shalt be with me in Paradise." It was strange that when she raised her eyes to the wall, they rested on that angelic face and form, traced there by the hand of De Vinci. To her it was a heavenly friend, who came to save. The smile on that beautiful face — so calm, so serene — was to her full of faith and love. This picture, taken from life centuries ago, nerved the heart of the poor flower girl, like the presence of a loving friend. It nerved her to stand firm and steadfast in the cause of truth and virtue.

She said : " Lady, you draw the picture of a world without God. A world that has no part in the goodness and loving kindness of Jesus. No, my dear lady, I want none of these things ; neither palace, gold, or fine apparel. They are suited to the noble and those born to fill high places. No, I will never forsake my parents, my Jean, and my humble life. My gifts of charity that I give to the poor and distressed are as pleasing to me as the costly gifts bestowed by the hand of wealth. My heart says, — You have done your duty ; you gave all you had to give. No, no, my lady, the happiness that comes from those I love, is not the enchantment of an idle dream, but real, true, and perfect in its joy. Oh, how I delight to be with my parents and my friends, in our humble cot, and look out upon the sea, the hills, and the beautiful landscape. So bright and cheerful it is for me to hear the sweet songs of the birds, and the glad, joyful laugh of the working peasantry, and when I can say to my own heart, the good God has done all this for thee and thine in loving kindness."

Lady Verono cast upon her a look of contempt, remarking, —" I have nothing to say, except that you are very simple and foolish," and left the apartment.

IV.

THE VOICE FROM BEHIND THE TAPESTRY.

IN this world, where there is an endless warfare between good and evil, if a sin is committed that is unpardonable, it is when vice, armed with wealth and power, tramples on virtue, and smiles upon the wounds it has inflicted.

Lady Verono was gifted by nature with brilliant talents, combined with a beautiful person. The shrine of virtue in her soul had been demolished and consumed by the fires of hate, malice, and ambition, or she would have fallen in adoration before this grand image of virtue and piety.

Iphi now found herself a prisoner, surrounded with splendor, and those beautiful objects which charmed her so much when they came as the offering of friendship: when offered her as the price of virtue, they were hideous, save alone that lovely face so full of faith and love; and although a silent witness of her sorrow, spoke of hope and consolation.

Often Verono came to her prison-chamber with apparent friendship and interest for her welfare; but in this there was no consolation or hope for Iphi, for it was too plain that she had betrayed her with some evil purpose in view, which Iphi could not at present discern.

Soon Count Vilani was introduced to her presence, and with his shrewdness and tact, acquired by experience in these cowardly acts of villainy, assumed a manner and air of truth and friendship, and Iphi was for a moment thrown off her guard by the wily seducer. He passed towards her, took a seat by her side, and said in most affectionate tones, —

"Iphi, you are so beautiful, that I cannot live without you. I love you, and all I have, this palace and all this wealth, I will share with you, and you must learn to love me."

"Count Vilani, this is impossible: nothing can induce

me to forsake my parents, nothing can induce me to cast aside my friends, to accept even an honorable life in this palace; and sooner than submit to dishonor, I would welcome death as my best friend."

"I am told," said the Count, "there is one who loves you; some base born peasant presumes to aspire to the love of one who should be the wife of a nobleman. Your parents shall be well provided for. I have had them already informed of your safety, and not to sorrow for your absence. As for this lover, I will have him sent to the battle-field, and you will no longer be troubled with him. No, Iphi, you must be mine, and mine only. See how grandly the Lady Verono lives. So admired, feared, and worshipped. You shall be placed above her as far as your beauty and loveliness is above hers. My Iphi shall be exalted above Verono."

Iphi replied: "This cannot be. The base peasant, as you call my Jean, and who has my love, and who has a right to aspire to my hand and heart, has never been appointed or decreed a nobleman by the king. God made him noble. He is worthy of my love and affection. Far sooner would I wed this base peasant, as you call him, than to wed you with all this grandeur and wealth. Fortune has placed in your hands power to defend and protect the poor and oppressed. How sad to think that you should be the first to commit acts of cruelty among the defenceless poor. What! love you, and discard Jean? God would forbid it. Sooner would I perish."

"Why, brave girl, you but increase my love, my passion. I am resolved to subdue you to my will. This night, when the cathedral bell strikes the midnight hour, in this apartment, a holy priest shall unite us in the sweet bonds of

marriage, and thou shalt be the Lady Vilani. Submit to
destiny ; it is thy fate."

Here then was the abyss in which they had planned to
cast her soul ; to despoil her of virtue by a mock marriage.
How horrible the thought. The deep schemes of Vilani
and Verono were now terribly apparent. In agony of
heart, with piteous tones, she plead with Vilani, to have
at least compassion for her aged father and mother ; they
would die broken-hearted ; that she never could return to
them except with that spotless innocence she possessed
when first beguiled into his power. "Pity me, for I am
nothing but a poor peasant girl, while you are a great nobleman, and can wed with one who can far better fill this grand
position of the Countess Vilani. Have mercy upon me, for
the time may be near at hand when thou shalt ask mercy
of others. The cruelty you now inflict on me may soon
return to you."

"Iphi," he said, "I love you and cannot part with you.
I am to be pitied."

Iphi stood confronting him. She was still clad in her
humble, modest garb of the flower girl. She had the
armor of truth and virtue ; she looked grand and majestic. The heartless Vilani for a moment trembled in
her presence.

What a mockery of this grand attribute of the heart for
the libertine to say to virtuous innocence, "I love you!"
Perhaps when the generous emotions of the soul are perverted by a life of crime, the base, selfish passion that
seeks to gratify its own desire is mistaken for love.

Jean's love for Iphi exalted him. It was Iphi's happiness that brought joy to his heart. It was the grand salu-
tation of love to joy. Love and joy met and embraced.

Virtue seeing this sweet union of love and joy, blessed both, and crowned them with bliss.

Vilani's love debased him. It brought as tribute to the altar, desire, jealousy, and crime. It was born of vice and darkness, its offspring, misery.

Vilani could have, with cruel jealousy, put Jean to death, for his love of the object of his desire. Had he loved Iphi in truth, and sought her love for her sake, for her happiness, Jean, with his noble soul, would have loved him.

Louis Dejon, generous and true, was Jean's best friend, because he sought with earnest solicitude to promote the happiness of Iphi.

Vilani's love was like the perversion of the charity and mercy of the cross into bigotry and hate. It was changing the joy which perfect liberty brings, for the woe that despotism offers.

The one was Promethean fire kindled at heaven's altar, the other was the consuming flames of the angel of darkness.

When she heard the words, "Iphi, I love you, and cannot part with you," the words "I love you," were revolting, and appeared to give her nerve to resist this villainous outrage upon her person, to thus imprison her, and thus force her to a union that would blight her life and bring unutterable misery and woe. There was an impressive look on this noble girl when she had resolved to die rather than be dishonored.

Gladly at this moment would she have accepted the altar of sacrifice, the cord, knife, flames, rather than the altar of marriage with this base fiend, who had betrayed her into his power to destroy her, both body and soul.

"Base, cruel man; you ask me to love you while planning my ruin. How could I love you?"

Vilani looked upon her with astonishment. He supposed he was dealing with a common peasant girl, who would soon yield to one of his commanding position.

He rushed towards her to clasp her in his wanton embrace. At that moment there rang through the apartment the stern words, —

"Beware! Beware!"

"What can this be?" Quickly he called Geno. Geno answered the summons.

"Geno," he said, "some enemy is lurking in the palace. Who can it be?"

"My lord, no one has entered the palace; who would thus dare to intrude?"

"Well, Geno," call Joseph, and search well in every nook and corner, and find, if possible, who is thus acting as an enemy and a spy upon me."

They all left the apartment, and poor Iphi sank exhausted upon a seat.

Lady Verono concealed behind some tapestry, near the front entrance of the apartment, had witnessed this interview between Vilani and Iphi. With feelings of anger and contempt, she heard the words of Vilani, "I will place my Iphi above Verono." She said to herself, "No, no, my Vilani; never will you reach the hour to place a mistress in the palace to rule over Verono." When Vilani rushed to embrace Iphi, she thought her plans might be frustrated, and changing her voice so that she could not be detected, she uttered the words, "beware, beware," and silently glided out into her chamber.

After making a full search, neither Vilani, Geno, or

Joseph, could discern any person concealed in or about the apartment, so that this affair was still to Vilani, a strange mystery.

He went in person to Verono's chambers, and found her resting on her couch in profound slumber.

V

MIDNIGHT HOUR.

The time designated for the consummation of this marriage ceremony had arrived. Here was the apartment in this palace. Here was heaven's livery, designed to give sanctity to holy bonds of marriage, to be used in the perpetration of the crime of crimes.

Here a priest clothed in the sacred robes of the high office of God's servant on earth. There the alter, the burning tapers, the Holy Book, in which is written the life of the man of sorrows, yet a life, replete and perfect, in the virtues of charity, and mercy.

The obscure outlines of the apartment, the solemn air and dignity of the priest, the dimly burning tapers, the subdued light of the chandelier suspended overhead, the midnight hour, the deep measured tones of the cathedral bell striking the hour of twelve, — gave to the scene the gloom of sacrifice, instead of the joy of marriage.

It promised the joys of marriage, but was designed as the sacrifice of virtue, and innocence. There is the altar and here the victim.

Iphi had hoped that relief would come before this crisis in her fate would be upon her. She had prayed in vain.

She stood now upon the very verge of the horrible abyss that had for so many long, weary hours threatened to engulf her.

Often had she asked her hard-hearted persecutors to pity her, to have mercy on her. They were unmoved by the tears of pleading innocence, and she yielded in hopeless, and helpless despair, and became in their hands, a passive victim to work out their cruel will. They had robed her in costly apparel. Vilani spoke to her words of comfort and consolation.

In this hour of sorrow there was still left to her one ray of hope. When she was led to the altar, she fell upon her knees before the priest, and said, —

"Holy man of God, have mercy on me and save me. All earthly splendor and wealth to me are as nothing without love and virtue. Nothing in this world so dear to me as my mother's love. Do with me as you will, but do not rob me of virtue and honor. Far sooner would I die."

Her heart was so full of anguish, the tones of her voice so full of touching pathos, that even these ruthless persecutors paused in their work of iniquity.

This poor flower girl, humble, unprotected, pleading with the representatives of a family of high and noble birth, who dwelt in a lordly palace, surrounded with all the splendor that wealth and art could bring to adorn, to have mercy, and spare to her a life of purity, and humility, was a touching picture of the grandeur and majesty of virtue.

Flashes from the cross of Calvary filled her soul with divine inspiration; and she was the personification of everything that was beautiful, grand, and noble in mankind.

She says, "You hesitate. Are there none to pity, none to save me?"

These words had scarcely passed her lips, when Paul Lorraine advanced and confronted Count Vilani. It was his manly form and dauntless bearing. He was crowned with the majesty of justice.

He said, "This innocent girl asks for pity, for mercy, you will not grant to her even that. I ask for nothing; I came here to demand a release of this helpless victim of your cowardly cruelty."

Vilani looked upon Paul Lorraine with derision. He said, "What presumption for a base-born peasant to enter by stealth the palace of a nobleman and command him to obey his will! I will teach thee courtesy, at least," and quick as thought, whipt out his sword from the belt and made a deadly thrust at the heart of Paul, who, with consummate skill, warded off the blow.

Geno sprang and grasped Paul by the shoulders, and the next thrust from the sword of Vilani would have been fatal; but Louis came like the bound of the leopard, saw Paul's danger, and struck Count Vilani on the breast with a stiletto, and he fell bleeding to the floor.

Iphi was bewildered with surprise, joy, and terror. Jean flew to her rescue, and with the assistance of Louis and Paul they carried her away from the place where she had suffered so much, and now all appeared like the awakening from a hideous dream.

Geno was about to alarm the servants of the palace, and then to flee after Paul, Louis and Jean, and arrest their escape. Verono said, "Stay, Geno!" The priest had left the apartment when the violence commenced. Verono and Geno were alone in the apartment. They went to the prostrate form of Count Vilani, who was bleeding profusely; and yet the wound did not seem to be mortal. He soon regained his senses, and in a low tone of voice requested Verono to send for surgical assistance. She gave him a cold, heartless look.

"Oh, Verono, I am dying: do not look so cruel upon me. Pardon me; forgive me; have mercy, and pity me."

"Oh, why? The peasant girl is not only beautiful, far above Verono; but she is also a prophetess, for no longer than yesterday she said to you, 'The time may not be far distant when you may ask for pity and mercy and it be denied you!' With her rare beauty, she is also able to foretell events. It is not surprising that you would place your Iphi far above Verono in this palace, and make a descendant of the Medici a base serving maid to a low born peasant girl, because she has a pretty face."

Count Vilani uttered the words, "Oh, pity! forgive and have mercy on me," and fell back faint with the loss of blood.

Verono said to Geno, "The supreme moment of my life has come; do now my bidding, and any request you make of me shall be gratified."

Geno sprang upon the prostrate form of the unfortunate Vilani, grasped his throat and held him until he had ceased to breathe.

VI.

The Two Sacks of Gold.

For the present we leave Vilani to his tragical fate and return to Louis, where he was confronted by Alonzo in the waste room with the two sacks of gold in his possession.

His first thoughts were of Iphi and this sad defeat of his plans to save her. Paul and Jean knew that he had entered the palace by the secret way, but could do nothing to help either Iphi or himself from this perilous position. He stood detected in the commission of a crime that involved his life. He was a robber. He had entered this mansion at the midnight hour by force and violence. These reflections to him were appalling in the extreme. He had resolved, however, to use no violence except in defense of his life.

Alonzo says to him, "Put up your weapon ; you are in my power, and escape is impossible. I have taken the precaution to fasten the panel by which you entered. It is not my desire at present to injure you if you convince me that your presence in this mansion is not for an evil purpose, but for a good purpose."

Louis was much surprised by this declaration, and promptly answered that he did not come here for the base purpose of taking this paltry gold ; that the gold was a mere pretence to save an innocent girl, who had been betrayed into this palace and here detained for purposes of the darkest villainy, and he was here solely by the promptings of justice and mercy to save her from dishonor.

Alonzo then asked him how he had obtained entrance into the palace.

Louis then related to him in full the agreement he had made with Geno to carry off this money, and that Geno was to divide with him Joseph's share of the stolen gold.

"Then you were concealed in the passage and heard the conversation between myself and Lady Verono. If so state what you heard as near as possible. If you are candid with me I will assist you ; if not, I will have you arrested here, and the consequences to you will be the loss of life through the tribunals of justice. Is not your name Louis Dejon?"

"That is my name. I heard in that conversation the name of Paul Lorraine. I heard you state that the false marriage was to be perpetrated at the hour of midnight on to-morrow. I also heard it stated that Francisco Vilani's death involved the crime of murder, and committed in this palace."

"Were you not examining that picture when you first came into this room?"

Louis answered promptly, "that he had been."

"Now listen to me. Swear by your God and your hopes of salvation, never to make use of the facts which I will relate to you, to the injury of either Vilani or Verono, and I will also assist you to secure Iphi from dishonor, and also save Vilani from a crime more detestable even than murder."

Louis answered : "I swear never to betray your confidence or to say anything that may injure you or your friends. I came here, not for the purpose of finding out family secrets, but for the sole purpose of rescuing that poor girl from a cruel fate."

"Then you will be silent on the death of Francisco Vilani.

"He possessed immense wealth. The vain, ambitious and licentious lives of Vilani and Verono are artfully concealed by the glitter of wealth from the eyes of the world. They could not await the death of this unfortunate man, but in order to have full control of all his possessions, all his great treasures, consisting of gold and diamonds of great value, they used this wolf in human form, Geno, to end his days by slow poison. They had no fears that Geno would betray them. His interest kept him still, and he knew himself that his looks and actions would have no possible influence with any one, and for him to attempt to tell his story would insure his swift destruction.

" My position in this household is one of great peril. I dare not interfere in the least with their designs. I do not desire, either, to have them convicted in a court of justice and die a disgraceful death.

"Did either of them know that you were in this mansion, and possessed of these facts, your escape would be impossible ; your death sure and swift ; your body cast into a vault, and if the officers of the law attempted to investigate through your friends, they would soon be silenced, by gold and false witnesses, to swear that it was impossible for you to enter the palace at midnight, or they would prove that you came to steal this gold, and that Geno killed you in the very act of robbery. Fortunate was it for you that it was I who detected your presence, and am here alone with you. Take this gold with you. Do with Geno just as you agreed, so as to avoid any interference with our plans. He is a cunning villain, and will quickly detect you if he sees that gold was not your object in entering the palace. Take this key for the postern gate ; this for the entrance to the secret passage. When you arrive on the second floor of the palace, to your right on the platform there is what appears to be a panel in the wall ; this key inserted in a small aperture at the base of the facing of the panel moves a spring, and the panel is easily moved back. You enter a passage, the first door on the left hand side leads you to the apartment where this mockery of marriage will take place. Be there with Paul

Lorraine, Jean Gendron and yourself in that passage, so that you can enter the chamber when the Cathedral clock tolls the hour of twelve. This may result in the death of Vilani, or yourself, or friends; but it will save this poor girl from cruel sacrifice. If you are compelled to use a weapon in self-defense, disable or disarm Vilani, but spare his life if possible."

Louis closed his lantern. Alonzo led him to the secret passage, opened it, and Louis departed to seek Paul and Jean, and relate to them the strange turn of fortune that took place in the palace of Vilani.

Geno was so busily engaged the next day, obeying his master's orders, that he did not find time to seek Louis to get his gold and a return of the keys to the postern gate and secret passage. He seemed, however, satisfied that Louis had the gold, and would act in good faith with his friend, who had introduced him to so valuable a treasure.

It brought supreme joy to the heart of the gardener and his wife that their precious child had been restored to them. With tears of gratitude they thanked her deliverers and earnestly prayed to the Infinite to bless them.

VII.

Geno makes Joseph promise to Return the Gold.

The morning after Louis had carried off the concealed gold, Geno says to Joseph, "How is our money, Joseph? was it all safe and secure when examined on yesterday evening?"

"That it was, Geno; all right, my good comrade; al' right."

"I have not gazed upon our shiners for some time, Joseph; let us go to our hidden treasure, and enjoy the sight."

"Go thyself, good Geno, go thyself."

"Why not thee go with me, Joseph? I should think it strange if thee refuse, and think you had done something amiss when last you had handled those precious sacks."

Accordingly they went to the place where their money was concealed. Joseph removed the rubbish, but the money sacks were missing.

"What is the matter, Joseph?"

Joseph was amazed. The sacks of gold were gone. Geno looked upon him with a stern and threatening manner, saying, "Base villain! thou hast robbed me. I doubted thee when reluctant to come to look upon our gold. Now I see by that guilty stare upon thy face, cursed villain, that thou hast taken and hid my sack in some other place to rob me. Confess, and tell me where they are, or I strike you dead where you stand."

"Geno, honest Geno, if I hope for salvation and pardon of my sins, I have not taken the money."

"Thou liest, base wretch, and thus to rob a friend. It was I who told thee of the place where money could be got, and thus you repay me for my kindness. Come, confess or I will kill thee."

"Have mercy, Geno. I took not the gold. I will swear by the Holy Cross and all the saints that I took not the gold."

"Joseph, then thou wouldst add perjury to thy many crimes. This is dangerous gold; it has been stained with crime — now thrice stolen. And now, guilty wretch, thou art willing to damn thy soul to perdition, by swearing to a lie upon the Holy Cross. This I will do with thee ; swear by the cross and saints that in one month's time thou wilt have this loss made up to me."

" I swear, good, noble Geno, to have it here in value, either in gold, jewelry or precious stones. I will truly do my best to make this right with thee, my good and generous friend."

"Well, see to it, villain. I will keep an eye upon thee, and if I find thee false thou hadst better never been born. If you did not steal this money yourself, where can it be ? How do you say it has been taken away ?"

"I have but one thing to say, that about the midnight hour, while you and I were on the watch below, I heard footsteps and low conversation on this floor of the palace, and knowing it to be Alonzo and the Lady Verono I said nothing, as it was of no importance, and was not any part of our duty to make note of it."

"Do you think, Joseph, they could have found the gold, or is this but an idle story of thine to clothe acts of villainy with apparent innocence, and to wrong thy good friend of his honest money."

"Geno, I am innocent ; but as I live I shall make it good to thee, and restore all you have lost."

BOOK VIII.

MUTINY.

I.

Forgive me, my brain was on fire
And I knew not what I did.

PAUL LORRAINE rejoiced at the deliverance of Iphi, yet
to him the ending was tragical and sorrowful. He regretted
that Louis had been so hasty, for he believed that he could
have cast Geno off, and warded the thrust of Vilani's
sword, and saved the shedding of blood. Louis assured
him that his blow was not necessarily fatal, which was
true ; for Vilani's life would have been saved with surgical
aid, and the flow of blood stopped. If he had lived, however, with his wealth, power, and influence, Paul, Jean,
and Louis, could not have escaped his vengeance. Paul
saw the sombre shadow of evil falling on his pathway.
We all feel at times as if under the hand of destiny. This
mysterious connecting of events in human life seems beyond our vision. Our happiness is so often disturbed by
what others have done. Let any one examine his past
life, and he will see small, unimportant events, changing
his entire life, and having a direct bearing on the fate of
others. This appears more mysterious to us, when the
fate of nations is changed and effected, by what appears
trivial and unimportant. Victor Hugo, in his matchless
description of the battle of Waterloo, gives a very striking

illustration of this. Blucher asked a peasant boy the road
to Waterloo. Had the boy said, take the left instead of
right, Blucher would not have reached the battle-field in
time to have saved Wellington from defeat. Napoleon,
victorious at Waterloo, would have changed the map of
Europe.

A ship is lost at sea, valuable lives and cargo all sink
beneath the ocean wave. The human mind can form no
idea of the vast amount of evil that event produced to
many thousands of human beings, running through hundreds of years. Suppose Columbus with his ships, his
men, and his enterprise, had been lost at sea, and left no
vestige of this wonderful event in the history of the human
family. Could any mind, save the mind of Omnipotence,
form any conception of the consequence of such an event
to the whole human family?

If Joseph had been devoured by wild beasts, as his
brothers had represented to Jacob, his father, and the
blood upon the coat of many colors had been the blood of
his beloved Joseph, the children of Israel would never
have suffered Egyptian bondage; Jacob and his descendants would have dwelt forever in the land of Canaan.
Pharoah's daughter would have never preserved the life
of the infant Moses. He would not have evoked the
thunders of Sinai; he would not have written the com-
mandments; he would never have led the children of
Israel out of the land of bondage, into a land overflowing
with milk and honey; and we would not have been informed in the nineteenth century, after four thousand
years had passed away, that Moses — the founder of that
wonderful people of ancient and modern times — had
made many blunders and mistakes.

These wonderful and startling discoveries in science, philosophy, and astronomy, appear to us often as the result of mere chance, while they are the logical result of a chain of events, directed by an Infinite intelligence to their final development. We see the result, and yet the motive or the designs of the Infinite mind in adopting these modes of development, is far beyond our grasp or comprehension. It leads us to this conclusion, that in the womb of future there are still grander developments to spring from the Infinite mind, to startle and astonish mortal man with his power and wisdom.

II.

THE next morning at the usual hour the regiment to which Paul and Jean belonged was out on parade, when a sergeant, with a file of soldiers, came from the headquarters of the commander, demanding the surrender of Paul Lorraine, Jean Gendron, and Louis Dejon, charging them with leaving the garrison against express orders, and breaking into the palace of the commander at the midnight hour, for the purpose of robbery and murder.

Paul, Jean, and Louis, all promptly came forward, willing to surrender up to proper authority, and have these charges investigated. The entire regiment demurred to the surrender of these men to any of the servants or friends of Vilani. The officers on both sides were consulting as to the proper authority to investigate these charges. Every man, almost, in the regiment felt convinced that if these men fell into the hands of their enemies their doom was sealed. Unfortunately for all concerned in this trouble, some one concealed in one of the angles of a building near by, fired at Louis,

The ball grazed his head and killed a soldier in the ranks, standing back of him. Louis saw the person who had shot, and he believed it to be Geno, and that he was preparing to fire another charge. He rushed toward him. Paul followed, then Jean. A large portion of the regiment, smarting under repeated acts of petty cruelty, and understanding pretty well the origin of the charge of robbery and murder, followed Paul, Jean, and Louis.

The officers made every effort to prevent this movement. Their commands were disobeyed. To add to the unfortunate condition of things, the file of soldiers that came to arrest Paul, Jean, and Louis, fired on the advancing ranks, killed and wounded several of them, and then fled to where the main body of their regiment was stationed.

Paul Lorraine afterward said, "I knew not what I was doing, for my brain was on fire." He was enraged to that degree that his judgment and self-control were completely gone. The ordeal which he had passed through for the last twelve hours, in witnessing the most cowardly villainy, drove him to a condition of frenzy. He led ; the regiment followed, and every man who resisted the movement was driven from the garrison. He and and his followers were in absolute possession.

It is said that the calm follows the storm. To Paul Lorraine this calm was one full of terrible reflections. He knew full well that, as far as his acts were concerned, in the rescue of Iphi, he could have been easily vindicated ; and that he had acted according to the promptings of right and justice. But alas, here was an offense of an entirely different character. He had led these men into

an act of mutiny and insubordination, that some one
would have to answer for with life. There could be no
pardon for such a breach of discipline. To let such an
offence go short of the severest punishment all order and
discipline in the army of Italy would be at an end. The
emperor himself could not allow such a flagrant act of
mutiny pass without some marked degree of punishment.
He might himself be pardoned, either by the king of
Naples or the emperor, but it would be cowardly and ig-
noble for him to escape and allow the men, who followed
him to protect him, suffer instead. This thought was more
bitter to him than to die. He said to himself, "I have
disgraced the army of France." To him this thought was
agonizing. He had crossed the Alps with Napoleon, and
had performed his duty so well, so nobly, and so bravely,
that the great commander had congratulated him with
kind words and smiles of approval. He was in the battle
of Marengo, and fell bleeding in the righteous cause of his
country. He was in the battle of Jena, where the army
of France confronted the grand army of Prussia, and
achieved an imperishable fame. He was now passing
through gloomy desert ways, and drinking the bitter waters
of despair. How dear was his mother and Annetta to
him at this time. The words of Annetta that he was good
and brave, and no harm would come to him, and that the
good angel would find him out and lead him out into the
paths of peace and happiness, added to his sorrow and
grief. And yet he did not accuse himself of crime. He
asked himself what fiend had led him into thus violating
a duty to his country. He bravely resolved to die, if his
country demanded this as an example to maintain the
order and discipline of the army of France. Ready was

he to make the sacrifice by offering all he had to offer in this world — his life.

His heart went out to that far-off home in the Alps valley, the happy, joyful scenes of his youth. There was his mother, his wife Annetta, his uncle Louis and all his dear old friends. There still was the grand mountain-cliff with the dark green forest at its base, the warbling brook, the cottage home, the small, well-cultivated fields and vineyards, the Briançon road, the little cemetery reposing in the shadows of the pines and cliffs, where sleep the beloved dead. At this hour the peaceful landscape was smiling beneath the rays of the rising sun. The birds singing their morning songs in praise of the God who ever looked with tender compassion upon the sorrows of the children of men. In this dark hour of his fate this scene of joy and happiness was to him but a bright, glad dream of life, that was soon to vanish from his sight forever.

When Paul Lorraine thus reasoned in his calm moments, when this storm of passion had subsided, and left this wreck of his happiness, and the peace of those he loved so well, his estimate of his situation and perils when Napoleon was heard from proved correct.

III.

Geno.

The news upon the streets of Leghorn the next morning after the death of Count Vilani, was that the villainous Geno had led three soldiers into the palace for the purpose of robbery; that Count Vilani while defending his

life was disabled by a blow from one of the robbers.
Geno, seeing that his master had detected him in his villainy, murdered him to conceal his crime, thus hoping to
escape punishment. But it was fortunate for justice that
the Lady Verono saw him commit the deed, and fled to
save herself from this terrible monster who had murdered
the kind friend who had fed him and protected him for
years. It was also stated that Geno was in prison awaiting his trial before the tribunal of justice.

It was also stated that an attempt was made to arrest
these three soldiers, and they being protected by the regiment to which they belonged, fired upon the officers sent
to arrest them. And thus it was that the whole regiment
stood in open defiance to the established authority of the
garrison and were guilty of mutiny, and that when the
emperor and king of Naples were informed of these
crimes they would be punished. The next day the Lady
Verono had the officers of justice ordered to the palace.
She stated that she left Geno alone with Count Vilani,
and fled in terror to her own apartments. They examined the body, and it was found that he had died, not
from the wound on his breast, but from strangulation, and
evident marks of a bloody hand were found on his throat.
These circumstances pointed to Geno, and they went to
his room and found that he had changed his apparel,
which showed that when he had the unfortunate man by
the throat his knee was on his breast, and there saturated
with blood. There was, of course, evidence of other acts
that led to unpleasant inquiries that did not suit the
countess; and as these faithful servants of the public
desired, above all things, to act in accordance with the
wishes of one now so wealthy and powerful, they humbly

rested, and were content to drag the villain off to prison, to answer for his crime before the tribunal of justice.

When Geno appeared in the morning he congratulated himself on his success. He had not yet received the gold from Louis; but that was sure, as he had the confidence and friendship of Verono. Those words of hers were charming — "Geno, obey me, and all thy wishes shall be gratified."

When the officers of the law arrested him, and said, "You are charged with the murder of Count Vilani," he smiled and said, "Surely this is but a little pleasantry thou art playing on me."

They showed him their authority and order of arrest. He then begged to be taken to the Lady Verono, but was informed that the lady was so distressed at the death of the count, that she could not see any one, and sent Geno word that on the day of trial she would be present, and aid him to the extent of her power. His cowardly heart trembled for a moment, but he gathered courage again by assuring himself that it was not possible for the Lady Verono to betray him into the hands of the law, when he was but the instrument in her hands in the commission of this crime, and other crimes in this palace.

This artful rogue had lost his cunning. When Verono had bribed him with promises to commit the deed they were alone; what good for him, with his villainous looks, to charge the countess with being his accomplice in crime? What would his word be against the now powerful and wealthy Verono? Nothing. The people, the officers of justice, would laugh at him, jeer him, scoff him, call him lying dog. Thus, when in his cell, these thoughts came into his mind, and he concluded he was in the snare.

Yet better keep a silent tongue, and rely on the generosity of Verono to save him, who had been so useful to her in her career of ambition.

The wily villain, with all his cunning, had not the wisdom to see that because he had been useful to her in a career of crime, to gain her present position, was the sole and only cause for her seeking his destruction, and, like the assassin, would wish to conceal the tell-tale dagger, covered with the life-blood of the victim he had destroyed. The success that comes of cunning, instead of wisdom, brings with it the seeds of its own destruction.

Count Vilani's remains lay here in state, ready to be conveyed to Florence, to be deposited in the family vault, to lay down in death among his fathers, some of whom have slept there for centuries. In a few days they were removed, with all the pomp and ceremony of so distinguished a personage.

He is beyond both the praise and censure of mankind. Well is it for the memory of erring man that the tomb covers our faults, if it does not speak of our virtues. It is a pleasing reflection, that we all feel towards the dead a desire to forget and forgive their faults, and enlarge on their good qualities.

When we have sympathy for the condemned on the scaffold, or confined in the walls of the gloomy prison, we do not sympathize with his crimes, but sorrow for his misfortune.

IV.

MURAT, KING OF NAPLES.

THE emperor Napoleon, when officially informed of this unfortunate mutiny, was aroused to the highest pitch of anger. His orders to Murat, king of Naples, were imperative and wrathful. "No court martial. Put to death every man engaged in this violation of order and discipline if you decimate the entire regiment."

With the emperor, there was no offences so unpardonable, as those that led to demoralization of the army. What he disliked most in this affair, was the national aspect, it had assumed ; bad feeling between the French and Italian soldiers. He punished with instant death the man caught in fraudulent acts in the commissary department. Shoddy contractors and commissary robbers found no safe place in the army of France, under his control.

It was these inflexible laws, and the prompt punishment of everything that led to demoralization, that made the order and discipline in his army almost perfect ; and kept his army united and powerful.

It was this kind of discipline, introduced into the army of Prussia by Frederick the Great, that gave it its marked superiority even up to the present day.

When Joachim Murat, king of Naples, received the emperors orders to punish this mutiny with such severity, he was struck with consternation and dismay. He knew that many of these soldiers had shared with him both danger and hardship, on many a battlefield. He was attached to the soldiers by feelings of pure affection. Oftentimes, he had said, that he hoped the day would never come when his duty would compel him to issue an order to have a French soldier put to death. The day had come, and brought with it sorrow and regret.

He proceeded to Leghorn to obey the orders of the emperor. The regiment was assembled in the garrison to receive him. His stern and commanding presence, the severe tones of his ringing voice, with his fiery, impetuous manner, struck the entire regiment with terror. He repressed his feelings of sympathy, and stated to them the imperative orders of the emperor, and said, that his duty to his country demanded that these orders should be enforced to the letter.

The regiment was now confined in the garrison and sent a deputation to Murat, to ask for clemency and mercy ; swearing that they would die on the battle-field under the very eyes of the emperor. Murat's heart, with this appeal, was touched with pity and mercy. Well he knew that every man in that regiment would consider such a death acceptable under any circumstances. At length he said to them, in tones of compassion, " I will accept three, to be chosen by the regiment in such a manner as they may determine, to die for the rest ; and thus make an example that no such breach of discipline in the army of France can go unpunished. And I will thus far take upon myself the responsibility of modifying the orders of the emperor."

The regiment being in the condition in which we have described, Paul, in the cool hours of reflection, when the brain was not fevered with the wild passions of hate and vengeance, saw with clearness that their offence could not be wholly pardoned without some example to deter others from such mutinous conduct so demoralizing to good order. They received Murat's order of clemency with feelings of gratitude. They at once proceeded to make arrangements to cast lots, for the three who were to suffer death, to atone for the rest. Paul Lorraine stepped forward and said that he was prepared to die, and that he had finally resolved to suffer the penalty of his own folly, in allowing himself to be betrayed into this mutiny. He said there would be no joy, no happiness to him, to live, with such bitter reflections that he had led any fellow-being to such a fate. Jean Gendron stepped forward and stood bravely and manfully by his side. Then came Louis Dejon, last, though not least in those qualities that make the real and true man. The soldiers who stood around these brave, dauntless men, were moved with deep compassion, and the entire regiment was in tears.

When Murat was informed of the action taken, and these three men had offered themselves to suffer death on behalf of the regiment, it added to his regrets. The act had something so grandly heroic, that the king of Naples was moved with intense feeling. Gladly at this moment would he have renounced crown and sword if he could with duty say to these brave men, " You are free."

V.

THE SENTENCE.

At the solemn hour of midnight, Paul, Jean, and Louis, were conducted before Murat, King of Naples, to receive the sentence of death. He said to them, " To-morrow evening, near nightfall, outside the Pisan Gate, on the

glacis, you will be shot.   I know you are brave men, and
are willing to die.   France asks of you this sacrifice.   It
was noble in you to offer your lives, thus to save others
equally guilty; but it is the only way for you to wipe from
memory, dishonor to your names.   I rejoice with you that
you are so noble, in your last hours.   I rejoice with you
that you are so heroic, to accept death rather than
dishonor.   I will charge myself with the duty of transmit-
ting your last farewells, your last regrets, to your fathers
and your mothers.   Have you thought of your poor
mothers?"   Sobs stifled their voices   "These poor women
would have been proud of you, had you fallen in battle
confronting the enemies of France.   It is unfortunate
that you should die thus.   It will be a consolation to
them to know that France demands a sacrifice to save
the discipline and order of her Grand Army; and that
you were so heroic and brave as to say, we are prepared
to die for our country.   Your parents shall not want
for support while I am able to assist them.   A good
priest shall be with you to offer all the consolation of religion.   Think of God, your country, and your mothers;
you no longer belong to this world."

They cast themselves weeping at the feet of Murat, not
to ask him for pardon or mercy, but that they might have
forgiveness before death from their commander, whom they
loved so well.

"Poor souls, I forgive you.   I pity you, and could
weep with you."   They were conducted from his presence.
He could no longer restrain his emotions of sorrow.

VI.

Iphi and her parents had been alarmed for the fate of Paul, Jean, and Louis, from the first time they had heard of this unfortunate mutiny. The news of the death sentence, almost paralyzed the heart of Iphi when she first heard it. They had rescued her from a fate worse than death; and that noble act was the cause of their misfortunes. This made her sorrow intensely bitter and hard to endure. She had compassion even on Count Vilani, as cruelly as he would have wronged her.

There was no despair, or wailing cries in her sorrowful plaints, but the outpouring of tenderness and tears of a grand heart, that saw infinite love, away and beyond the dark shadows of earth's gloomy pathway.

She wept and sobbed, and said, "God will be with them when they pass through the valley of death."

Despair never comes to the grand soul that feels in the hour of agony, that God is still present with infinite love. Tears may flow, the heart be steeped in pain and grief, yet there is still that shining star of faith, that ever beams bright, clear, and radiant, with the golden promise of God's love and mercy for mankind.

Even nature opened her lips and spoke to her. Why so concerned about death? it is but one of the natural phases and conditions of the immortal life of the human soul.

Amidst her tears she would say, in broken sobs, I must not weaken myself with sorrow, I must keep strong, now, and not allow this sad event to break me down, for God has given me a duty to perform, to care for and provide for my dear old parents, when in the infirmities of age.

She nerved herself and went to see Paul, Jean and Louis, for the last time.

The meeting between Iphi and Jean was most pathetic and touching. Her love for Jean was strong and enduring, for she loved him for his virtues of truth, sincerity, and justice. She bade them all a final farewell, and gave to each love's parting kiss on earth, firmly believing that she would meet them all in a better world beyond the grave.

The king of Naples had made an investigation of this affair at the palace, and Vilani's death, and regretted very much that he had not been informed of Col. Vilani's despotic conduct over the garrison, as he would have removed him and prevented this calamity.

He heard of the meeting of Iphi and Jean, and was touched with pity for their sad fate, and sent for Iphi, hoping he could speak to her some words of consolation.

He told her he was aware of the cruelty that was attempted to be perpetrated upon her, and the part these brave men had taken to rescue her, and that it nearly broke his heart to condemn them to death. Maiden, they are not stained with crime, they are dying like true, brave heroes. That he would gladly save their lives if he had the power. That he had written to the emperor the modification of his order to punish all engaged with death, by accepting three to suffer for all.

" I regret, maiden, that your friends offered themselves instead of drawing lots as I suggested. Yet I honor them for it. They die now in honor, not in dishonor. They die a glorious, heroic death, and in all my life in the armies of France I have not witnessed grander acts of heroism.

Do you understand me, maiden, in what I say, and my position?"

"Sire, I do understand what you say, and O, how my poor humble heart thanks you for this kindness. And I know, sire, God will bless you, and I will pray for you all the days of my life; and my good old father and mother will pray for you, pray God to bless you in this world and in the world to come."

"Maiden, console yourself with this reflection, that Joachim Murat, king of Naples, will record the truth, that these brave men died in honor, not in dishonor. And I say in conclusion, that I would resign all positions in life, if my duty and honor to France would allow me to set them free."

"Oh, sire, how I thank you for these words."

"Now, dear girl, farewell; and when you need a friend apply to Joachim Murat, king of Naples."

Iphi departed to convey these good words of the king to her parents.

On the day of this unfortunate occurrence, Paul had taken the precaution to write to Annetta and his mother, in order to prepare their minds for the worst. After he was sentenced he wrote the sad intelligence with sorrow and tears. He plead with Annetta not to mourn and grieve over him, but to kindly remember her dear Paul. He reminded her that her mother needed her care and consolation, and recommended them both to the care of good old Uncle Louis, and gave his last farewell to his dear friends.

In a few days the king of Naples will write you a letter of condolence. He concluded by saying, farewell wife and mother, the best beloved of all the earth, we surely will meet in heaven.

VII.

The Execution.

It is the evening of the 19th June, A. D. 1808, well
on towards nightfall, and these three unfortunate soldiers
of France are to suffer death, to maintain the rigid and
inexorable laws of military discipline, in the French army
occupying Italy.

The shadows of the hills are cast far out on the sea;
the earth, the waters, and the air, and the busy hum
of commerce, on the mart of Leghorn, are all silent in
this solemn, twilight hour, as if uniting in a few brief
moments, to pity these victims of misfortune, who so well
deserved a better fate. The golden light of the setting
sun still lingers on the sea, beyond the long shadows
of earth, as if it would fain light their pathway through
the valley of death. See! there comes out of the wide,
open gate of the garrison, a regiment of soldiers, march-
ing to the tap of muffled drums. At the head of the
regiment, inside of a hollow square, is Paul, Jean, and
Louis, on the way to execution. How silent, how solemn,
with heads bent, and flags draped in mourning, they
march along, with slow measured step. They are veterans
who passed through the fire at Marengo, and the flames
of war at Jena, yet every cheek is moistened with
tears.

They march along through the wide avenue, lined on
either side with mansion and palace, towards the Pisan
Gate, and many a kind heart in these mansions and
palaces are throbbing with pity for the unfortunates; for it

THE EXECUTION (near Leghorn, Italy).   Page 122.

has gone forth that the king wept when he condemned them to death.

They pass though the Pisan Gate, and halt upon the glacis. A platoon of soldiers is marched out of the ranks.

Each one of the condemned is placed at the head of his coffin, twenty paces from the platoon. The sergeant having the execution in charge takes each one by the hand, kisses him on the cheek, and says, "Farewell, brave men, are you ready to die?" The answer is in the affirmative. The word to fire is given. They fall, are laid in their coffins, and are carried to the cemetery on the hill for interment. The regiment is marched back to the garrison, and this sad drama of life is closed. Night comes with her shadows, and silently falls on land and sea. The shining stars are soon out with radiant splendor in the clear, blue sky; there they sparkle in countless numbers, with a transcendent glory far beyond and above all the grandeur and glory this dull earth has to offer to the admiring gaze of mortal man. They are eloquent with a language that speaks of infinite goodness and wisdom. They sing the song of praise to that God who, the humble mother of the Alps valley said, "In the end maketh all things well." The dawn of the next day disclosed three new made graves in the cemetery on the hill, overlooking the wide, open sea. They lay side by side. Alas, for thee Annetta, and for thee Iphi! The days of joy that are past and gone will never return. Good is it for both, that thy faith is steadfast; that there is a blessed One in heaven, who tempers the wind to the shorn lamb, for this world has no consolation adequate to thy bereavement.

BOOK IX.

I.

TRIBUNAL OF JUSTICE.

THE day appointed for the trial of Geno, for the murder of Count Vilani, arrived. Tribunals of justice, in States under imperialism, clothe themselves in all the paraphernalia that inspires awe and terror. When the criminal is on trial, the executioner is present with some insignia of his office. The judge assumes far more the looks of the avenger than the merciful. This is, perhaps, the case in all governments that are ruled by imperialism. They wish to have the people look upon their rulers and masters with fear and trembling. In republican governments, the judge exacts respect by a dignity that arises from a proper appreciation of his truly important position. He is not the enemy of the unfortunate man who stands in his presence on trial for his existence, but the true, merciful friend, who sees to it with ceaseless vigilence, that the presumption of his innocence, which the law throws around every one, is not removed until it is proven beyond a reasonable doubt that he merits the punishment which the law has affixed to his crime.

Geno had all the time relied on the hope of the assistance of Verono to save him in the last hour. When brought into the presence of his judge, with the officers of the law as his accusers, even with his evil appearance, now so friendless, so unprotected, with the stern, defying, and threatening look of the judge and accusers, it is strange that even Verono was not herself moved with at least some pity for the poor wretch.

The countess and Alonzo appeared as witnesses. Geno had an advocate to defend him; paid and selected by his enemies. The officer of police testified to the marks on the throat of the deceased; that the wound on the breast was not the cause of his death, the mark of the bloody hand on the throat, the blood on his clothes where the knee had been placed on the breast of the dead, his guilty looks and actions. Some questions were asked as to the persons who entered the house and made the assault upon Vilani; but a look from the court silenced all inquiry upon that subject.

The lady Countess Verono, came forward and testified. The court was all humility and obeisance to her ladyship, while Verono repaid him with one of her most gracious smiles.

"What does your ladyship desire to state with regard to the prisoner?"

"Nothing, my lord; except that when this dreadful encounter took place in the palace, I fled from the room in terror, and sought safety in my own chambers, under the protection of my attendants."

"Will your ladyship state if you knew anything of the whereabouts of Geno, when you left the room?"

"Nothing, my lord; except I left him alone with Count Vilani, and knew nothing of the matter until the next morning, my attendants finding it necessary to soothe my disordered, nervous condition with powerful narcotics.

"I was very much shocked with the lamentable and tragic ending of Count Vilani, while attempting to force this innocent girl into marriage. Alonzo and myself made every exertion in our power to persuade him from it, but all in vain. At length, from pure pity and compassion for the girl, we had enough of her friends introduced into the palace to rescue her, and carry her off and injure no one, and had it not been for the unfortunate interference of Geno, all would have been well; the poor girl saved, and the life of a nobleman preserved."

Geno, at best had a villanous look, but now his face was absolutely hideous. It was livid with rage, agony, and resentment. He turned to speak, but his throat sent forth a horrible and unearthly sound. The judge promptly silenced him with a command, "Silence, guilty wretch!" He looked at the executioner, and he returned the look to Geno, with an angry scowl that made him tremble. He saw now his doom was sealed; the gibbet was before him, with all its horrors. He saw there was no hope, no pardon for him; he realized with dismay that Verono had planned his destruction to conceal the evidence of her own guilt. He again and again tried to speak, but was stunned with a blow from an officer.

Alonzo and Verono were politely excused from further attendance upon the trial. After their departure, the court, in a solemn and awe inspiring manner, condemned the unfortunate Geno to death. He was immediately carried to the ball and ironed, and on the next day he suffered the extreme penalty of the law.

II.

THE BEGGAR.

Seek and ye shall find,
Knock and it will be opened unto you.

Sometime after the events of the last chapter ; towards night-fall, when they were about to close the City Gate leading out on the glacis, there passed out of the city a beggar, clothed in the ragged garb of poverty, the cast off raiment of some nobleman. He was old, infirm, and very wretched. His form was tall, and bent with age. His features were cadaverous, and blotched with dark, pallid spots, while his eyes burned and glared with either fanaticism or insanity.

He would have been hideous, were he not grotesque, or grotesque if not hideous.

No one seemed to notice him, except some kind ones who gave him alms. They perhaps had seen him oftentimes and knew him well.

He had under his arm a sack in which were some crusts of bread and meat and gifts of charity given him by some kind good heart that had pitied his misfortunes. He walked bent, and used what seemed to be an old worn out spade as a support to his tottering frame.

The sky was dull and leaden in its aspect, and covered here and there with blotches of inky clouds, except along the western horizon there were long lines of gloomy crimson light, the last reflections of the setting sun. Had you followed after this man in the darkness and noticed him when he reached the summit of the hill, between you and the glimmer of the horizon, you would have noticed that he no longer walked bent, but was standing erect and turning himself around as if looking for something.

He passed down the hill, on the opposite side, and was now crawling on his hands and knees, along the inside of a broken wall, the remains of some ancient structure that had long since fallen to ruins. There were some old stunted trees, that grew by the side of the wall, and from his action you would suppose that he was measuring the distance these trees stood the one from the other, and how far each tree stood from the wall. The broken spade is no longer a walking stick, but is used for the purpose designed. What is the beggar doing? Surely he must be looking for concealed treasure. Perhaps he is no beggar, but a robber, who hides in this deserted place his stolen goods.

He has now found the object of his search. It is placed in his sack and slung over his shoulder, and it being now quite dark he assumes an upright position, and gropes his way out of the ruins.

III.

Not far from this place is the dwelling and home of Iphi and her parents. At this very hour they were talking of the sad fate of their good friends. Iphi still has that cheerful, contented smile. She is not broken down with sorrow, for she knows well that her duty in this world is still to struggle, and bring happiness and contentment to the living. She has not lost one particle of her energy and industry to procure every comfort for her dear parents. She loves to dwell on the memory of her dear

Jean, and believes that in the other world he is happy, and cared for by One who is able to bless him with a joy far above all earthly kindness, and that in the world to come they will be together again, never more to separate.

They were at this time, praising and blessing Murat, king of Naples, for his generous and noble bounty. He had heard of the conduct of Jean, Louis, and Paul, in rescuing Iphi from the villainous plot of Vilani. He purchased for them this cottage and the grounds, upon which were planted their vineyard, their garden for flowers, and the small fruit orchard. He gave them to understand, that the death of these brave men was no dishonor to their names and memory, — that France had demanded some sacrifice, so as to save her armies from demoralization, and these brave men came forward, and offered up their lives to save others who were equally to blame for this unfortunate calamity.

Murat, agreeable to his promise, had written to Mother Lorraine, in substance what he had written to Iphi's and Jean's parents, and as well to Louis' parents, who resided close to the same place, to see that none of them were in want for support, as long as he had the power and means to aid them.

While they were conversing of these things, there was a step at the door and then a gentle knock. Iphi said, " Come in !" The door slowly opened, and the beggar that we saw passing out of the Pisan gate, stood in the doorway. In the full light that fell upon this man, his face was more haggard and care-worn, his garments more tattered and ragged, his step more feeble, and his body more bent than when first we saw him. Everything about his miserable appearance seemed to say, I am poor; pity me, help me!

Iphi said to him, "Poor man, come in. This house is ever open to the poor." He sat down on a seat, and laid his sack on the floor. The old spade he had perhaps concealed or thrown away.

Iphi had frequently seen this man on the streets, and at the market-place in the city, and recollected seeing him several times at the gate of Vilani Palace, talking to Alonzo, but who he was, or from whence he came, she knew not. Iphi kindly asked him if he needed help in any way.

He said in reply, "I came not to beg: I am present in this house of prayer in the name of God, to bring gifts to the poor." His earnest manner, strange, wild appearance, and above all, that terrible energy that flashed in his eyes, and was apparent in the deep, earnest tones of his voice, carried conviction to the hearers that he was in earnest in what he had said.

He continued in the same impressive manner. "In the midnight hour, an angel of God came to me and said: 'You know where there is gold that has been cursed with crime; you need it not. In the hands of charity, it will be a blessing to the poor, and thus atone for the evil it has wrought. There is in your midst, one whose heart is full of the grandeur of Jesus. It is Iphi. The Greek flower girl. Take it to her in the name of God, and with her it shall be blest in deeds of charity, and mercy.'"

This scene was so strange and solemn, and this statement of the appearance of the Angel, and the words spoken, that all were inspired with reverential awe. The beggar rested his head on his hands in an humble attitude, as if in prayer.

Iphi at last broke the silence by saying that for her to be in possession of gold, would make people talk evil of her, that it was not honest that she had so much gold to give to the poor.

"What matters it, noble maiden. God knows that thy heart is pure and truthful, and full of loving kindness."

Iphi was still fearful that some evil would come of this, but what could she do? Was this some temptation, or was it some move to entrap her into peril and danger? She could determine nothing; she knew not what to say.

At length she spoke to him. "If I refuse to accept this gift would you take the gold with you when you depart and use it yourself in purposes of charity?"

In a firm voice he said, "No; it remains when I go hence. I obey the orders of my master. I dare not take it. When I go, it is without it. You can return it to no one, no one owns it. You know not now, nor never will in this world know, who brought this gift to you. The Infinite has given you this gold for deeds of charity and to save the lost and ruined. You need never attempt to discern from whence it came, or who I am; for never in this world will you know. Accept it and use it; for it is the will of the mighty one that you should do so."

He thrust his hands into the sack and drew out two sacks of gold. One fastened with a string the other with a piece of fine wire.

He arose from his seat, placed the empty bag under his arm, and said, in a solemn voice, "May God ever bless the dear noble hearts who dwell beneath this roof, where abideth love, charity, and mercy, and is exalted far above the palace where pride, vanity, and ambition, hold licentious revelry."

These good people entreated him kindly to stay until the light of morn would show him his way.

He said nay, and passed out into night and darkness and they saw him no more. It was very evident that nothing whatever would change this man from his purpose. Any one to have witnessed his appearance, his words and actions, would conclude that he was acting in compliance with what he firmly believed to be the command of God.

Now, what were Iphi and her parents to do with this gold, evidently a large amount in value? It was to them a novel position, and that night there was earnest prayer for divine guidance. They sat it away in a safe place with the intention of awaiting events, and perhaps something would come to light, and explain the mystery.

The father and mother both suggested to Iphi to see Alonzo, and perhaps he could give them some instructions what to do. Iphi now recollected that she had herself given this beggar small pieces of coin as alms, and had seen others do it; and how was it possible that he could have all this gold honestly. Yet his sincerity and earnest truthfulness seemed beyond question. If he had stolen this gold as a robber, why should he bring it to them to give to the poor. It was a mystery, and they concluded not to use it until they became convinced that this money was honestly his to give away in deeds of charity.

IV.

AMBITION'S TRIUMPH.

The lady Countess De Vilani, was now the star of fashion. The picture she drew to allure the humble Iphi was marked with poverty in comparison to the actual splendor and extravagance of her own present life. She seemed to be ambitious to cast in the shadow the princely style of royalty. Her equipage and attendants were queenly in their style and numbers. The world, or at least the fashionable part of it, worshipped her with adulation and praise. They said, We adore her for her proud, lofty spirit, her great ambition, and above all her splendid fortune and success, and the possession of all the things in this world that can be desired to make one happy and prosperous.

She paid these sycophants and flatterers well for sounding her praise. She added greatly to the adornments and style of the palace, and there she gave them fete after fete, with the most lavish expenditure. These festivals at the Vilani Palace were the admiration of the nobility far and wide, and it seemed as if the Countess De Vilani was far from being any discredit to the grand fame of her ancestors, the wealthy and powerful Medici.

At these festivals, all ablaze with light and splendor — her classic features, elegant form and magnificent apparel — she looked the very queen of beauty and fashion. She possessed the most consummate skill in address, and acted well her part that every one would exclaim, "What a charming lady is the Countess?" With all this success, these votaries of pleasure at her very feet, this immense wealth, great talent, personal beauty, surely the Lady Verono, Countess Vilani, must be supremely happy. There are now no living witnesses who can bear testimony to the dark secret of her life, except the quiet, retired Alonzo, who she but seldom sees or thinks of, as he takes no part in this dashing life of pleasure. From him, therefore, there is no danger, and besides he knows of no crime except the one in which he was himself an accomplice.

There was no witness to the part she took in the murder of Vilani, except Geno ; and her scheme for removing Count Vilani and casting Geno into the pit had succeeded, and left no evidence of crime against her.

She had no God to fear, for as Iphi told her, she dwelt in a world that had no God, and took no part in the loving kindness of the Jesus she loved and worshipped. Therefore she must be happy, for all her wishes were gratified, crowned with success, and she the proud, triumphant mistress of her own destiny. What more is there to kindle the flames of ambition? Nothing. Then is she truly happy and content.

There are times when mysterious moans come out of darkness, as if violated justice was struggling for utterance and vindication, and no one to hear her or to answer her demands. It is one of the convictions that sometimes exist in the public mind and heart that is ever struggling for utterance, and yet cannot find expression to declare its judgment.

The vast show of wealth, and the magnificent display in the present life of the Countess De Vilani, revived the old gossip of the secret disappearance of Francisco, the insane cousin. It found its way among her friends and admirers. They would often want the countess to know what sincere friends they were to her, by denying the accursed slander, and again and again these tales would come to her ears, until there was a secret dread in her mind that perhaps some one had witnessed the dreadful part she took in the murder of the count.

The talk among the gossips and news-mongers in Leghorn now was that the Countess De Vilani, had been by some unknown persons, most cruelly slandered in being accused as an accomplice in the crime of the murder of Francisco, and these slanderers had better beware or they would be severely punished for such baseness towards the noble countess.

The story now afloat and current and not denied, was that Alonzo and Geno were the guilty parties, that there was positive proof among some of the servants in the palace, living here at the time the crime was committed, who stated that they knew that Geno carried the poison and gave it to Alonzo, and that he administered it to the unfortunate Francisco.

These charges, not being denied by the ardent admirers of the countess, became more positive and direct. The quiet and amiable Alonzo was not disturbed by these accusations, although oftentimes informed of them. This calm indifference of Alonzo to these positive and direct charges of a crime so heinous, with a penalty so terrible, was to the countess strange and unaccountable.

She could not silence these tales, but found to her terror, they increased instead of diminished. There was no telling where they came from. No one knew, or could tell. No one knew why the people believed in such a thing, nor had they ever heard any one say any thing positive about it. To add to her uneasiness about this trouble, there was a perceptible change in Alonzo. He was more thoughtful, and absented himself more from her presence. He was more punctual in attendance on the confessional, and at times, would slightly speak of repentance, and atonement, and being sorry for acts committed in the past. There were times she thought it possible, that when Geno made his confession of guilt at his last hour, he might have included her in his confession, as participating in his crimes. Yet she knew that this was not the source of the public gossip and talk, that was constantly coming to her ears, and so repugnant to her feelings. The powerful and wealthy countess found to her regret, that her frowns would not even silence the gossip of Leghorn, let alone all Italy.

Could it be possible that Alonzo was, through his infatuation on repentance and making atonement, betraying her to her ruin. These reflections, running in her mind, kept increasing her anxiety to find out the true origin of these reports, and with one bold act, set them at rest forever. She had lost none of her daring and courage, but the idea of a public trial, condemnation, and a disgraceful death on the scaffold, was to her pride horrible in the extreme. To be tried in a public tribunal of justice, as Geno was tried, and so condemned, and so executed — she could not for a moment endure the thought of such a ghastly spectacle.

If perchance some daring one should charge me with the crime, and drag Alonzo into court to testify, how would this simple being act. This new-born fanaticism of his in the cause of Christianity and piety, and confession, for the sake of pardon for his sins, would drive him to sacrifice both me and himself, to save his soul from the flames of perdition.

The penitent Alonzo will yet prove more dangerous to my safety and security than the villanous Geno. Fool that I was, that I did not clear them all away from my pathway. Can I use this talisman (looking at the ring on her finger with the serpent's head)? The danger at this time, when the public mind is full of suspicions against

me, would render such an act dangerous and full of
peril.

Francisco Vilani, it can be proved, died in Alonzo's
charge, and when they were alone, Geno carried the poisoned food, gave it to Alonzo, and thus he was, in fact, the
actual perpetrator of the crime. How can he connect me
with his guilt. No one except Geno or Vilani could have
done that. Then I have it. I will forever wipe this slander from my name by having some friend charge Alonzo
as being the real perpetrator of this crime, and send him
after Geno. He will become penitent, confess his crime,
and die willingly, and thus the public mind will be put at
rest forever on this troublesome affair that mars my pleasure and enjoyment. I will think of this ; it seems my
best and only plan.

If he must die, the deed must be done by myself, for I
will have no more witnesses. Let me reflect.

First the report was current, that the Countess De Vilani was strongly suspected as an accomplice in the murder
of Francisco. The act would have an ugly look.

Her friends had started the report that Alonzo was
alone the guilty party, as Francisco died while alone with
him, and in his special charge.

This changed the current of opinion, and it came to
light that there were witnesses in the palace who knew that
Geno and Alonzo were in fact the guilty ones.

Then Alonzo dies suddenly. The conclusion will be
poison, or that he had committed suicide. Perhaps it can
be made to so appear. But this plan of throwing the
crime on Alonzo, has brought to light the fact that Francisco was murdered by Count Vilani's confidential servant,
Geno.

Then why is Lady Verono the head of the household, enjoying this wealth? How is it possible for her to escape with these facts proven. There is but one way. Have Alonzo charged with the crime in the tribunal of justice; prove that he and Geno committed the crime, that no one else knew anything about the matter, that Alonzo reported him dead, and that he died in his sole charge.

Thus I am resolved to remove Alonzo from my pathway. And I will use the law to work my ends, and thus, in the end, be the supreme mistress of this household, the mistress of my own fate, the architect of my own fortune.

V.

ALONZO.

SHE determined at length to question Alonzo on the subject, and ascertain if possible his views and intentions, and see if he in any manner suspected her of having any part in starting these accusations.

Accordingly, at her request, Alonzo was informed that she wished to see him in her apartments, on matters of importance. Alonzo, prompt to answer the request, appeared in the presence of the countess. His manner and appearance was more humble and obedient than ever. His look was much more care-worn and anxious than usual, and if possible, more quiet and reserved.

Countess.—Good day to you, my faithful friend Alonzo. I have not had the pleasure of your company for some time. Why so distant and reserved of late.

Alonzo. — You can be assured my lady, that it is not that I am indifferent to your welfare and happiness, for that is vastly more important to me than any other consideration in this world.

Countess. — It has grieved me of late that the gossips of Leghorn are so unjust as to charge you with crime, and to drag before the public gaze the old forgotten slander of the cause of the death of the unfortunate Francisco.

Alonzo.—I am willing to meet my fate, be it what it may. I am in the hands of the Infinite, who is above all, and worketh out his own will. I am ready and willing to stand before my accusers in the tribunal of justice. If condemned by the laws of my country, I am willing to suffer. It is my destiny. So be it, if it is decreed that I shall suffer. Human life is wrapt in mystery. We cannot judge God's motives or designs. We cannot say to him that this and this is right, this and this is wrong. But we can place ourselves in accord with him, by taking to our souls the lessons taught by Jesus and the prophets of old. ' Be charitable and merciful to all mankind, and unspeakable joy will come to thee in the end.'

Countess. — Well! well! Alonzo, you have been taking lessons from Iphi. I hoped that all this nonsense about humanity and charity, love and mercy had come to an end, and that you were prepared to meet your enemies face to face, with pride, courage, and defiance, and be true to the fame of your ancestors.

Alonzo. — My lady I fear not ; for myself, I am content. It is for you that my soul is troubled; it is danger that threatens you, that brings this gloom upon my heart.

Countess. — Fear not for me, Alonzo ; the only thing that I fear is, that some busy body may charge you with the crime before the tribunal of justice, and I be compelled to bear witness in the trial against you, which I would well desire to avoid.

Alonzo. — Fear not for that, my lady. I will confess to all my crimes that are true, and charged against me.

Thus the conversation ended. Alonzo departed, and the Countess Vilani sat musing intently on the strange condition of things, and the fearful part that threatened her very existence.

"Ah!" she said. "I have removed the least dangerous witness. Geno's villany and cowardice was far more safe than Alonzo's fanaticism and willingness to confess and suffer. I see my danger and peril.

"Soon he will conclude that, to save himself from the punishment in the future world, he must expose all. Let me reflect. Does he know of his own knowledge that I had anything to do with the murder of Francisco, accept as a silent witness of the act of Vilani by his servant Geno? Does he know that I induced Geno to close the career of Vilani? He thinks it, doubtless. He knows that I was instrumental in that affair with Iphi; but that can be explained, that I was coerced and driven into that by Vilani.

"He will not be likely to include me in his confession of guilt, only upon actual facts of his own knowledge. He will not expose me when guilt is only presumed.

"He says, 'It is for you I fear. I am not concerned about myself.'

"Can it be that he knows of the part I took in the death of Vilani? It must be so. I now see my danger.

"I must have some one to consult in this dilemma. Let me think over my long list of lovers, and admirers, and see who I can best trust. It must be one who is wealthy, and does not need gold. I need not confess my guilt ; I will but just hint to have Alonzo arrested, and have my name disconnected with this crime, by a decree of the law-tribunal. I can trust my best friend, the Marquis De Vaubert. I will get him to proceed in the matter."

A few nights after this, she had a splendid banquet in the palace of Vilani, and consulted the marquis in her private reception-room.

The marquis, with his keen perception, at once saw the design and the wish of the lovely countess.

The next day one of the marquis' willing, suppliant tools. charged Alonzo in the tribunal of justice with the murder of Francisco Vilani. He was arrested, and the day of trial fixed to appear and answer the charge of murder.

BOOK X.

LOUISIANA.

I.

CAPTAIN ETHAN ALLEN SMITH.

LOUISIANA at one time belonged to France, and was settled in an early day largely by French emigrants. The majority of the population of New Orleans, in the forepart of the present century, were decidedly French, who possessed that business tact, energy and enterprise of the same class of business men in Paris.

At this period, there was in New Orleans a commission merchant by the name of Pierre Lavasse, who was very prosperous and successful. His place of business was where most of the commission houses were situated, on the levee. Pierre was a Frenchman, pure and unmixed.

He came from Marseilles, and was exceedingly proud of his grand France, and the fame of Napoleon. He was an ardent, warm friend in the cause of liberty, and his constant wish and desire was that France should have a republican government.

When he heard of the downfall of Napoleon, and that he had been exiled on the island of St. Helena, the good, generous Pierre was moved to tears.

It was very sad and mournful for him thus to see the grand idol of his earthly adoration, in the power of his ruthless enemies.

Pierre was wealthy, notwithstanding his many losses, for he had a weakness in never refusing to endorse the

paper of his numerous friends. Every time Pierre lost
he had a particular oath. "By Jingo! I never sign him
again!" But Pierre being utterly unable to say no, violated that oath oftentimes. From the kindness of his feelings, he still signed, still paid, and would still swear. "By
Jingo! I no sign him again — sure dis time!" It never was
any consideration in these acts of kindness that he expected compensation, and yet to a very great extent he was re-
warded, for every one of any influence seemed to be interested in his prosperity, and his business was very exten-
sive and profitable. He had great redeeming traits about
him, he lived plain, substantial, and prudent.

Pierre had one friend that he would have endorsed with
his purse and life. It was Ethan Smith a Yankee sea
captain, who commanded a merchant vessel engaged in
trade between the Mediterranean ports and New Orleans.
His vessel was named The Lafayette of New Orleans.
Captain Smit, as Pierre called him, was the counterpart
of Pierre. He was continually boasting of the Yankee
nation, and on the question of the Rights of Man, they
were in perfect accord, and many a jolly bumper did they
drink together to the success and prosperity of their respective countries. Captain Smith was a brave, noble-
hearted Yankee sailor, and always on the side of the helpless and injured. He did all of his New Orleans business
with his friend Pierre, and had done so for years.

Just as soon as Pierre was notified of the arrival of the
Lafayette, he was on board to welcome his friend, Captain
Smith.

"Captain Smit, you came from de Meditteraneyon,
ha?"

"Yes, Pierre, I did; but I think the climate will be too

hot to return with a merchant vessel. John Bull, has commenced his bad tricks on American sailors ; and the States will bring him to task for this impudence, and take a little of the sea pride out of the old fellow, I am thinking. When the Lafayette goes to sea again, she goes armed, Pierre. How are the exiles, Pierre ? "

" Well, and hearty, Captain Smit ; good men ; very good men."

" All safe, Pierre ? Mums the word. You say they are good men."

" Yes they are good men. They are the best metal I ever saw put up in human shape. They are iron, and rock ; and true as steel."

" See here, Pierre. If I had some iron bull dogs on those decks, and some food to make them bark and bite, and had her manned with such men mixed a little with Green Mountain, damned if I wouldn't face any two ships John Bull could float on the seas. If war does come with the States and England, the Lafayette sails into the fight. I have money enough to spare to make her all right. All I will ask Congress to do, is to give me the iron barkers. She is a capital sailor, none better on the ocean. I swear by the gods, the Stars and Stripes shall never come down by American hands. When the flag comes down it goes with the ship. They sink together."

" Ah, Captain Smit, by Jingo I know you never surrender."

" Not much, Pierre, by Moses. I have some of the best French on board, Pierre. It is fit for gods and heroes, or men with big souls ; and damned if that don't fit you, Pierre. We will, drink on this our first meeting. to our first loves, the Tri-Color, and the Stars and Stripes."

" Yes, Captain, we must drink to that sure."

" Pierre, Napoleon is still uppermost fighting the kings. He is knocking them old thrones in Europe like foot balls. He will bring John Bull to terms before he finishes up. He has the best army ever organized. He has the best marshals that ever drew blade. He must let the States alone. He has the love of the people who are in favor of a republican government. If he attempts to play fast and loose, the people will mistrust his democracy; and besides that, we are able to give him some hard blows on the seas. He must hands off, on the Yankee Nation. By Moses, he must hands off. '

"Ah, Captin' Smit, Napolyon have very good soldier, and is one grand general ; but see, now, he never fight wid dis country. He friend to dis country. Pierre La-vasse, don wid Napolyon when he fight dis country; he will whip de English very bad."

Captain Smith said to Pierre: " I like the English well enough in their place, but, by Moses, they must keep their hands off these States, this side the big pond. My good old father was born in England; but I say this, if I was to tackle an English man-of-war, and my good old father was on the English deck, with British uniform, and under their flag, I would give the old man notice to go below deck, or by Moses, he would get hurt. See here Pierre, my name is Ethan Allen Smith. My good, old mother was a kin to Ethan Allen : and she was just like him, by Moses. My mother, God bless her, made cartridges in the war of the Revolution, and my old father shot 'em, and if his aim was as good on a red coat as on a deer in full sweep, the red coat went down, by Moses. Did I ever tell ye, Pierre, about Ethan Allen and old Fort Ti-conderoga? "

"Yes, Captain Smit; when we get a little dry, then you tell me about him, and see now, we go into cabin, take a drink, and den, Captain Smit, you tell him again sure."

"Well and bravely, Pierre."

"I was talking of Ethan Allen. He was solid timber — the tall pine that had stood the storms and blasts of many Varmont winters. In the war of the Revolution he got together some Green Mountain boys and says to 'em, 'I am going to yank the Britains out of old Fort Ticonderoga, and if you brave boys will follow me we will do the job up in quick time.' They answered him with a shout. They went and soon they scaled the fort, and took possession. The old commander of the fort was at the time snugly housed, thinking there was no danger from a set of wild, raw soldiers from the Green Mountains, and he thought he would turn over and take his morning nap. Ethan Allen says, 'I believe I will go and wake up the old gentlemen, and inform him what us boys have been doing.'"

Captain Smith's voice became a little husky, and Pierre suggested a little more of the brandy, so they took a drink.

"Well, now, Pierre, the balance of the event is soon told. He went to the entrance of this inner stronghold, and struck the hilt of his sword, against the iron bound door, and made everything tremble. The old gentleman could not rest under such a noise as that. He came to the door in his night-clothes, with a lamp in his hand, and there stood the tall, strong, and rough form of Ethan Allen, with his sword in hand. 'Who are you, and what do you want?' said the old Britisher.

"'I want you to surrender this fort!'

"'To whom, and in whose name, am I to surrender this fort?'

"'I demand possession of this fort in name of Jehovah, and the Continental Congress!'

"Pierre, by Moses, he was good timber, sure as you live; let's take a drink."

"Captain Smit, he was one grand man, sure; well, by jingo, we take a drink."

Captain Ethan Smith was a good representative of Ethan Allen, according to the description of that remarkable personage. He was physically strong, rough, rugged, brave, generous and noble, — loved liberty, and hated oppression.

"Captain Smit, I wish to say one thing; my business have increase, and I must have a good clerk, here on ze levee, and in ze office; what you say to dat captain?"

"You want a good clerk, Pierre? Do you want a man just coming into prime of life? A good penman? Speaks French, Italian, Spanish, and English? Has been several years in the same business in New York city? Smart as men are usually made? Far more honest, (true, and brave) than they are usually made, Pierre? A man who is as faithful and just as the exiled brothers, Frank and Claude Harrold? A man for whose worth and integrity I will put in pledge my word and honor?"

"My God, captain, where you get such a man as this what you speak of? Ha, by jingo, it is better zan I expects to find!"

"I have him here, right on this ship Lafayette."

"Where you get him, my good friend?"

"Direct from New York, Pierre."

Captain Smith rang a bell, and a negro boy came to the cabin-door, and he ordered him to bring Mr. Convors to the cabin, that he desired to introduce him to a friend.

When Mr. Convors appeared, there was nothing in his

personal appearance, except an easy, graceful temper, showing that he would readily adjust himself to any condition in life, to which duty called him, that would strike the observer on first sight. He was evidently a man that would wear well, and this Pierre Lavasse saw at once.

" Charley," said Captain Smith, "this is my friend Pierre Lavasse, the gentleman I have spoken to you about. Pierre, this is Charles Convors."

Pierre grasped his hand, and said, "Mr. Convors I want you for a clerk in my counting-house, and on this levee; I am commission merchant. You will suit me, for Captain Smit says so ; and he never makes mistakes in men, by jingo! He did make one mistake, when he fell in with Pierre Lavasse."

" That is true, Pierre, by Moses, for you are a damned sight better than I supposed you were ; now let us take a small drink on that."

" Well, just as you say, captain! Will Mr. Convors join us?"

" Excuse me, Mr. Lavasse, I never indulge in the social cup. I never use even wine. I hope you will not consider me unsocial. I refuse because I think it is better for me, and better for my friends, for I can perform my duty in life much better without it."

" Excuse you, Mr. Convors, excuse you, ha, by jingo! You goes into my counting-house, and command your own price. See, Mr. Convors, you commence this day. You marks on ze ledger the amount of your own salary. Do you understand me?"

" Yes, Mr. Lavasse, I understand you perfectly, and I am under great obligations to you. I will strive to do my duty, and serve you to the best of my ability; and as to salary, I will accept no more than is usual for such service."

"Pierre, when I invited you to drink, I did not include Charley. He never touches strong drink. Charley you are at liberty to leave us, if you desire to do so; perhaps you would like to take a ride or stroll around the city."

"Stay, Mr. Convors," said Pierre. "I must go up to ze house, and get things ready there for ze reception of my friend, Captain Smit, and his young friend. I will send carriage down for you, and then you can take ride around the city, do you see? Mrs. Lavasse, and my daughters will be delighted to receive you at ze mansion."

On their parting, it was understood that Captain Smith and his young friend were to go to the Lavasse mansion, and there to remain until it suited their pleasure.

That night Captain Smith and his friend were safely and snugly housed in the good, old, comfortable mansion of the Lavasse family. Mrs. Lavasse was a French lady of culture and refinement. The foundation of her character was remarkable good sense, and all of her actions were the prompting of charity and affection for every one with whom she was connected. When her husband invited any one to the mansion, she treated them in her kindest manner, with marked respect, without ever making an enquiry as to their opinions on politics or religion, or their condition in life. One would suppose that the rough, blunt, unpolished sea captain, with his "by Moses," and occasionally a little stronger expression, would be offensive to a lady of refinement. But it was not so. Her good judgment, clear discernment of character, saw at a glance that he was an honest, noble-hearted man. And she knew further that her husband would

never have become so firmly attached to him as a friend,
if he had been otherwise.

She was a living example of the fact that the only way
to secure obedience and good conduct, from the servants
or slaves in her household, was to treat them with the
greatest degree of kindness possible. She was neither an
advocate for slavery, nor was she in favor of their immediate, unprepared emancipation. This was her argument :
He who loved mankind with a charity that was infinite,
commanded us to be charitable and merciful to all mankind. What was the result of such a life? It drew
towards her the love and affection of all. Her happy
home was full of glad sunlight and joy. It went forth
into the world to cheer the hearts of others. The negro
slave, that was the absolute creature of her will, would
have died for her willingly and freely.

Mrs. Lavasse had two daughters approaching their
" teens," named Eva and Carolina. Eva was the elder of
the two, and they were both examples of the fact that kind
treatment of the child gradually and gently moulds the
young heart with love, truth and fidelity towards the parent.

Both Pierre and Madame Lavasse had been raised in
the Catholic faith, and what their opinions were on creed
or theology. I do not suppose that any person could ever
tell from their intercourse with the world, but there were
many that had felt the joyful influence of their putting
into actual practice the virtues of Christianity.

BOOK XI.

ON TRIAL FOR THE MURDER OF FRANCISCO VILANI.

I.

THE SACKS OF GOLD.

WE are back at Leghorn. We did not get here on board of the good ship Lafayette, sailing under the proud banner of the Stars and Stripes, under the protection of the brave, gallant Captain Ethan Allen Smith. We are here on the wings of thought and memory.

Iphi is still faithful in the performance of duty, still working for others with a cheerful heart. The days of her joyful love for her Jean, and sweet friendship for Louis, cling to her memory like a beautiful dream that has vanished, and left with her a memory that is full of melancholy pleasure.

Her parents are still living in the dear old home on the hillside. The two sacks of gold delivered to them by that strange man are still to them a profound mystery. Who was he? Whence came he? Whither did he go when he went out in night and darkness from that threshold?

Iphi says to her parents, I have never seen that man since. Although her father and mother had lived in, or near Leghorn for many years, they had never seen that man before the night he entered their humble cottage.

He had told them that they never could find out who he was, and that it would be useless to make search or inquiry. There was no effort on his part to disguise his face; his dress was that of the most abject poverty, and they naturally concluded that it was assumed, as he was evidently in possession of wealth to a great extent.

Where would they go to find him. Alonzo knew nothing of him. Iphi had made inquiry of him. She never again saw that strange, haggard face, so full of sorrow and sadness, yet so truthful and earnest, and that flashing eye so full of the nervous energy of frenzy or fanaticism.

She was positive that if she again saw him, she would remember him. "What shall we do, dear father, and you, mother, in this strange affair?" asked Iphi.

"Daughter," said the venerable father, "we will not make use of this gold at present, perhaps something will come to light that will disclose and direct us in our duty. If the good God has sent this man to us, he will in due time lead us in the proper course to pursue. I notice that these sacks of gold have been hid in the ground, for there are marks of that upon them." They finally set them in a secret place, concluding for the present at least to await events. When they moved it, however, there was a paper closely rolled and attached to one of the strings. They opened it and it contained in substance, what the man had said to them. "This gold is mine; I give it to you; in your hands it will be blessed. It has been cursed with crime by others. In your hands God will sanctify it, bless it, and thus it will atone for the evil it has done in the world." There was no name signed to this note, nothing to reveal the mystery.

II.

THE morning of the day set for the trial of Alonzo had arrived. There in that ancient hall, venerable and majestic with age, and the gloomy, heavy architecture of the Tribunal of Justice, sat the stern judge, with the power to turn the scales on the side of life or death.

This was the same tribunal through which Geno had passed on his way to the grave. It had the same awe-inspiring authority. Here were the grim attendants, who executed the mandates of the judge. Here the one who brought the prisoner ironed into court, from his gloomy cell. Here the one who carried him to the place of execution, and put him to death.

On entering the vestibule of this temple, on the morning of the trial of Alonzo, there sat, on one of the stone steps that led into the hall of justice, a strange-looking personage, clad in the garb of a pilgrim. His long staff and scrip lay upon the mosaic floor at his feet. It was the beggar we saw pass out of the Pisan Gate, and that carried the two bags of gold to Iphi, — gave them to her in the name of God, to be held in trust for the poor, and to be used in charity and the salvation of souls. His face had the same haggard and mysterious look. He represented in his apparel a different personage. He wore a slouched hat, and his hair fell down on his back in masses of gray. His person was enrobed in a long, loose robe, with sandals on his feet. The casual observer, would not, perhaps, have recognized him as the same person ; even Iphi or her parents would not have known him, unless they had scrutinized his features very closely. He paid no attention to any one that passed in or out of the hall of justice.

Alonzo, led by the officers of the law, with chains on his limbs, into this tribunal, did not attract from him the least attention. The elegant lady, Countess Vilani, with her attendants, Joseph, and his companions, who were to testify against Alonzo, passed in, and yet he did not notice them. His eyes were intently fixed on the floor, or looking off in space, meaningless and expressionless. Alonzo stood in that dismal enclosure, where thousands of miserable human beings had stood before, to listen to the decree that sent them to the grave. No eye, save the eye of the Infinite, could measure the amount of human agony and suffering, endured in that little enclosure, during the long centuries that have passed over this ancient edifice.

Alonzo still maintained that stolid indifference to his fate that he had all the time manifested. He was looked upon by the court and bystanders as a hardened wretch, that would soon meet his just punishment.

The Potent Seignior was all courtesy to the Countess De Vilani, who sat surrounded by her maids in attendance. There sat Joseph, who was now released from his contract to steal a sack of gold, to make good the loss of Geno. This Potent Court had annulled that contract by condemning Geno to death.

Joseph's testimony was positive and direct, that Geno procured the poison and gave it to Alonzo, who in turn gave it to the deceased. In this testimony he was sustained by one or two old servants of the household, who had detected the same thing.

The countess assumed an air of deep sorrow and regret over the sad fate of her dear friend, Alonzo, as she called him, while her feelings were exultant over the success of her plans of getting rid of the last witness of her crime and shame. She was a little disturbed, over the apparent indifference manifested by Alonzo, when his conviction and condemnation was so certain; but she concluded he was willing to die, and that he would not now expose her, either designedly, or through religious fanaticism.

The court, with a solemn voice and manner, asked Alonzo if he was prepared for trial. He answered, meekly, that he was.

The charge, in usual form, was read to him, and in substance charged, that between certain days and year, in the Palace of Vilani, he had put to death Francisco Vilani, then Count Vilani, by administering to him poison, and that he was guilty of the crime of murder.

" The court then asked him if he was guilty, or not guilty?

Alonzo replied, "I am not guilty, my lord, nor is any one guilty of murder; for Francisco Vilani, or Count Vilani, was not killed or murdered, but is still living, and within the sound of my voice."

"Wretched, guilty man," said the Seignior, "what means this folly? The procurator has, in this tribunal, the witnesses who will swear, direct and positive, that he was murdered by your own hands. That Geno procured you the poison, but that the crime was, in fact, committed by you."

" Most Potent Seignior, that they will so testify is true. They are honest in their statements. Geno did bring me poison to take the life of Francisco Vilani, but I detected his crime and intent, and saved the life of Francisco, and at this moment he stands in the presence of this Tribunal of Justice."

All eyes were turned, and there in the centre of the hall, stood the tall form of the pilgrim, with his long staff in one hand, and his scrip in the other, looking with amazement upon the majestic form of the Potent Seignior, clothed in his robes of office.

"Who are you?" demanded the judge, in a stern voice.

"I am Francisco Vilani, who died to the world, many years ago."

"Do you claim to be Count Vilani?"

"Titles of nobility, are but vanities of earth. If I deal justly and charitably with all men, God cares not if man calls me count or beggar. I would have been glad to remain unknown to the world, but a good man was to suffer death for destroying my life, when he had saved it, and thus I am before you.

"The Count Vilani whom Geno murdered in his last hour, called on man to pardon him, to save him, to pity him. Had he called on God, he would have been pardoned and saved. The Lady Verono and Joseph know me."

The court called on Joseph; he being the witness to testify against Alonzo, declared under oath, in presence of the court, that this was, indeed, the Francisco Vilani who was supposed to be dead.

The countess was then called upon to state her knowledge of this personage. She arose, and in a clear, distinct voice, said, "Potent Seignior, it is Francisco Vilani."

The judge then stated that it was passing strange that this man, who was supposed to be dead for many years, should be produced on the trial of a man accused as his murderer, and asked Alonzo why he did not state, when he was arrested, that Francisco Vilani was living.

"Potent Seignior, it is thus: If I had so stated, still would I have had to appear in this tribunal and make my defence good by witnesses. Francisco desired above all things to remain unknown. Nothing in this world would have induced him to have thus acknowledged his identity, except to save me from a disgraceful death. It is one of the strange features of his insanity, that he wants the world to think him dead.

"And further, my lord, I wished to publicly, in open court, forever put at rest the slander against the Countess Vilani and myself." When attention was thus called to the countess, there was observed a deathly pallor on her cheeks, that spoke of intense mental anguish.

The court intimated to Alonzo that he might proceed and explain the extraordinary result of this trial, and how it was brought about that he had saved the life of Francisco.

Alonzo thus proceeded : "Francisco Vilani lost his parents when in infancy. The only relations he had at the time, were the late Count Vilani, Verono, and myself. He was considered insane in his boyhood, and kept in close confinement, and treated as an insane person, and did not possess any legal existence. He was Count Vilani to the exclusion of every other claimant, and the owner of immense wealth. All this was under the control and management of the late count.

"In the course of time it was concluded to remove him to the palace, and place him under my care and management, where there was a private communication in and out, known only to a few persons besides myself. He had been under my care but a short time when I discovered that it was not absolute insanity, but an extraor-

ordinary decree of eccentricity. He had a perfect passion
for mingling with the world under assumed characters.
For instance, he would clothe himself in the most ragged
apparel, and go forth and beg for days; and every cent he
could gather he would carry home with him. The next
step would be to clothe himself in citizen's dress, and in
the character of a gentleman of benevolence, distribute
this money among objects of charity. He would also, at
times, go forth as a pedler, selling fruit, toys, and works
of art, and use the proceeds in the same manner. At
times, he would assume the dress of a pilgrim, as at
present, and distribute money among the poor and
destitute. When Alonzo spoke of his dress as a pilgrim,
he induced several persons to look toward the place where
the pilgrim stood, but he was not to be seen, he had disappeared as quickly and suddenly as he came."

"What has become of Francisco Vilani?" demanded
the court. The officers made search for him, but could
not find him, stating that he had been taken away by some
person in a carriage.   .

Alonzo, however, proceeded with his narrative. "He
had assumed different characters that he did not recollect;
but in all these fancies, and eccentricities, he believed
firmly that he was following the absolute, and unqualified
command of God, and was perfectly harmless, and was
really good, kind, and noble, in his thoughts and actions.
I was at first a little fearful of indulging him in these
wild freaks, but I found out that it improved his health,
and made a very marked improvement on his mind; and
I also concluded that his being confined in almost a
solitary cell, even from his infancy up to manhood, had
been one of the main causes of the unfortunate man's in-

sanity. He had never been allowed to have any communication with his fellow-beings. I found that when he was allowed to live with men, and was at liberty to act for himself, that there came to him a decided and marked improvement.

"I reported that the day was not very far distant when Francisco would recover, and would be considered nothing more than a very eccentric person, but far from being insane.

"After some time had elapsed, Geno brought a mixture, which he said had been prescribed for him by a very eminent physician, and that I was to give it to him in certain proportions. I did so, and soon found out that he was rapidly failing in health, and if not soon stopped, he would soon be in his grave.

"I accused Geno of the crime, and told him I had detected him in his purpose.

"This was stopped, and Francisco recovered. Soon I detected another strange change in his appearance, produced by the food brought by Geno. On one occasion, when this effect was very marked, Geno was present. I locked the door on him, and then said to him, —

"'If you do not tell me now what this means, and who is engaged with you in this accursed plot to destroy his life, I will kill you.'"

Verono heard this part of the statement of Alonzo, with terror and dismay. She said to herself, "He will yet betray me. He is now the master, and I the slave. Fool that I was, thus to put in motion this accursed trial that ends in my own ruin and downfall."

Alonzo proceeded : "Geno confessed, and gave me the name of his accomplice ; and as he suffered on earth for his crime, and is now beyond the reach of all earthly tribunals, I shall not mention his name.

"I told Geno I would spare him if he would assist me to make the world believe that Francisco was dead. He promised. I knew that fear of his accomplice on one side, and fear of me on the other, would keep him silent.

"I purchased a comfortable residence in a very retired place outside the city, and procured the assistance of a firm, and a reliable friend, to take charge of the house and Francisco.

"I told Francisco about all I had done. He understood the situation well, and it pleased him ; for he said he did not want the world to know him as Francisco Vilani, but a servant of God, looking after the poor and miserable.

"Geno, myself, and my friend, placed him in a coffin, and had him carried out of the palace to the house I had procured for his reception. The empty coffin was fixed in such a manner as to be easily taken to the cemetery and interred without any danger of detection.

"He remained in charge of his attendant without any danger of being recognized ; for there are but a very few persons in the palace that had ever seen him to know him as Francisco Vilani. While in and around Leghorn, there were none that had ever seen him as that person. He often visited my apartments in the palace disguised as a monk, pilgrim, or pedler. He was, as he said, in the palace on the night that Geno murdered Vilani, and gave as a reason for not interfering in the behalf of Count Vilani, that God was using Geno as an instrument of divine justice, and that he, Geno, would soon fall in the same manner by violence."

(The Countess Vilani had her face veiled. Her soul was writhing in agony and despair.)

Alonzo continued: "Francisco regretted very much that he was now compelled to go before a court and be identified as Count Francisco Vilani; that he would prefer to have the world say, Francisco is dead. But he very readily understood that the testimony was sufficient to convict me of his murder, and then he said if he thus allowed me to suffer a disgraceful death as his murderer, when I was his good friend, and saved his life, that God would cast him out from his presence forever.

"I, myself regretted this on his account, for I have discovered that the more his wishes are gratified and he has perfect liberty of action, the more reason he has. He never seems to have any desire whatever to injure any one. He is insane on the wish and desire to help every one.

"His attendant, Calvetti, has been very faithful and kind to him, and has been able, having plenty of means furnished him through myself, to humor him in all his excursions, always being near him and watching him without his knowing it. They often, however, drove around the country, Francisco being dressed in such a manner as would be consistent with his being in a carriage. He was often told that his face resembled a beggar or pilgrim, or monk, or pedler, that had but a short time since passed that way, but that did not annoy him much; he paid no particular attention to such remarks. As long as he was not known as Francisco Vilani, he cared nothing about it."

This strange recital of Alonzo, almost paralyzed the countess with horror. Francisco was alive. Had been present at the murder of Vilani, concealed behind the tapestry of the apartment. Had just stated that if Count

Vilani had asked God to pardon him and have mercy upon him, instead of man, his prayer would have been granted. She had been the cause of this accusation, in order to have Alonzo put to death to screen herself against punishment for crime, and it resulted in bringing to life the real Count Vilani, the actual owner of all this vast wealth. Alonzo was more than vindicated, and had all the time been her true and only friend, and had been shielding both her and the late Count Vilani from just punishment. He knew, of course, that she was connected with the attempt to poison Francisco. He knew that she had compelled Geno to murder Vilani.

Where, now, Verono, is thy pride, courage, and ambition, to turn aside the decree that condemns every human soul who defies the inexorable law of justice? Where, now, thy lordly palace, shining in splendor, filled with luxury, ease, and grandeur? It has passed away like a dream, and the place of execution, with all the ghastly horrors of a disgraceful death, is there instead. The gay crowd of fashionable flatterers and sycophants that were wont to gather around thee with smiles and false praise is changed into a low, vulgar crowd of howling demons, who mock you, and jibe you in your agony, while suffering the pangs of a disgraceful death. How sad to think, that you may stand where Geno stood, and die where Geno died.

In this dark hour of her fate, she thought of Iphi, so truthful, noble, and good. She remembered when she said to her, your faith in God is a myth, and like the worship of Isis and Jupiter, will pass away like a dream. She remembered, too, that Iphi said, that the faith, hope, and charity that came to the world through Jesus and the prophets of old, would exist as long as there was a human soul to love, to forgive, and pity fallen man.

Verono, so cruel-hearted, could no longer endure this mental anguish; she wept. She moaned so pitifully, that the stern judge and the grave executioner could not restrain their tears.

Alonzo is discharged, Verono is taken away by her attendants. The pilgrim has disappeared, and this melancholy scene is closed.

III.

I Told You So.

THE gossips on the streets of Leghorn never had so rich a theme of exquisite relish, as the facts developed in the trial of Alonzo for the murder of Francisco. The most of the wise ones knew all this years ago, and said, have I not oft told you so.

First Citizen. — Tush man; I have often told thee, Francisco was not dead, but was wandering around in the different characters so well explained by the good Alonzo. Ye have no memory to keep what is told thee.

Second Citizen. — Well, well! I will swear that never to this moment, have I heard it so stated.

First Citizen. — Tush man; thou art dull of mind, and also of discernment. Thus it was given out, that Francisco was insane and dead in law; and the dull, simple fools took the legal fiction for the fact, and said, therefore, Francisco was dead, and soon the shallow pates had him murdered. Tush man, thou art dull of comprehension, and must hereafter mind what is told thee.

Second Citizen. — Well! well! I have nothing more to

say, except, I have seen this strange-looking beggar, and often times, for pity sake, gave him charity, and I have have often times seen the same strange face in hermit garb, with staff and scrip, and the same as pedler, dealing in pictures and toys and trinkets, and yet I did not think the one man represented all these characters, and never did I dream of its being Francisco Vilani.

First Citizen. — Tush man, it comes from a want of discernment ; thou art stupid. To me it was all plain that it was Francisco Vilani.

Second Citizen. — Well! well! How is it they say that the lady, Countess Vilani, is just as guilty as any one, and that in the tribunal she was struck with conscious guilt ; what sayest thou?

First Citizen. — Tush man ; what folly ; surely thou art insane. Wept with conscious guilt? She but wept with joy, — kind-hearted countess,— in thus seeing her kinsman alive, after years of mourning for his death. You must live with the nobility to learn their ways. I served for many years as serving-man to an honorable marquis, and I thus learnt these things.

Second Citizen. — Well, I see thou art well learnt in these things. I did but tell thee what others said. Tell me this, why did Geno kill the Count Vilani? and why did not the countess call for help, instead of fleeing to her chamber, while Geno was murdering the count?

First Citizen. — Tush ; what foolish questions thou dost propound. Geno had his accomplices in the palace to rob and plunder. The count was about to kill the wolf, and he turned upon him, and with the aid of his companions, he killed the count to save his own life. Dost see into it?

Second Citizen. — It looks that way, indeed it does.

First Citizen. — Your other question is answered easier still. Dost think a countess has a voice like a milkmaid? She fainted and fell with terror at the dreadful sight, was carried to her chamber senseless by her waiting maids. Dost see it now?

Second Citizen. — Well, thou art very sensible about these things. It is a good school, to live with the nobility and learn their ways. They say that Alonzo was a cunning knave to keep Francisco travelling around as beggar, pedler, and pilgrim, while he used Francisco's gold to live at ease and have all these fine livings to himself, how is it?

First Citizen. — Tush man; hadst better keep a silent tongue on such matters, or it may fare ill with thee. Dost know the danger of thy slander of these people? If you do not, I give you heed to keep a silent tongue. Mind me.

Second Citizen. — I thank thee for the warning, for there may be danger in thus speaking of great folks. I think so, indeed, since you have told me of it, and will look to it. But how is it, they say that the countess was acting with Count Vilani, in that shameful act in beguiling the innocent, beautiful Iphi into the palace, to drag her to ruin and destruction. How is that, neighbor?

First Citizen. — Thou art at it again; tush man; why wilst give utterance to these idle gossips on the street, and say they say. Thou art a fool; ye have no discernment; dost not see it? It was all a piece of pleasantry, like an act upon the stage in the theatre, for the noble countess to amuse herself in the dull hours of palace life; hast no sense left? Good-day, good-day! I no longer wish to talk to babbling fools such as ye.

Second Citizen. — Good-day. Excuse me. I did but ask of one who well knew all these things. Good-day.

Citizen Giulia (meeting second citizen).—Good-day, Ignati; hast heard the strange news? Francisco Vilani was not murdered but the noble Alonzo has saved him, and yesterday, in the tribunal of justice, in defence of the charge of murder, he produced the living body of the supposed murdered Francisco.

Second Citizen (Whose name appears to be Ignati).— It is not strange to me, Giulia, for I have known it these many years. Gabuzzi, the grocer, has oft told me that Francisco was still alive, and wandering about the country as pedler, monk, beggar, and pilgrim. You see, Gabuzzi has served amongst the nobility, and knows their ways quite well, and can tell it quite glibly, you see; and I have been true and kept the secret well.

Giulia. — What! Ignati has received this news from Gabuzzi the grocer, who sells to the palace of Vilani, for the servants of the palace, spoiled groceries and tainted meats, and at double price? Gabuzzi art a vain, babbling fool; heed him not.

Ignati. — Thou art very sensible; Giulia, I will think of this; perhaps the cunning Gabuzzi, is but playing smart with me.

Giulia. — Heed not such babbling boasters. Ignati, I will tell you of this man. When Geno was alive, Geno was, with Gabuzzi, the perfection of honesty. When Geno was forsaken to his fate by the countess, he was the murderer of Francisco as well as of the count. When the Lady Verono, as it was whispered around the streets, was connected with these crimes in the palace, Gabuzzi was among the first to charge Alonzo as being the accomplice of Geno in the murder of Francisco. Thus it is, Ignati, wherever the Countess Vilani has cast her gold you will find many such as Gabuzzi to swear that she is all perfection. Good-day, Ignati.

Ignati. — Good-day, Giulia. Thou art truly sensible and wise. I will think of this, and will not listen to such as Gabuzzi. Now I have said to Gabuzzi, thou art smart and wise; also have I said to Giulia, thou art sensible and wise; and both have told me different tales of the palace folks. If they are wise, then I, Ignati, must be a fool. Well, well, I will think of this.

IV.

THE INSANE COUNT.

SHORTLY after the hermit was missed from the hall of the tribunal, a chaise passed out of the Pisan gate. It contained two persons, and took about the same direction the beggar followed when he searched for the two sacks of gold in the old ruins. It proceeded to the cottage on the hillside where Iphi and her parents dwelt.

Iphi and her parents were sitting in the cottage, talking of the sad fate of Paul, Louis, and Jean; of the terrible death of Vilani, and of the ordeal through which Iphi herself had passed. They had heard of the arrest of Alonzo for the murder of Francisco, but knew nothing of the trial and what its probable result would be.

A stranger came to the door who they supposed was a nobleman, who wished to purchase some flowers. The chaise stood at the gate and the driver still sat in his seat.

There was something about the face of the stranger that startled them all very much; for it had the same strange, haggard, vacant gaze that marked the beggar who left with them the two sacks of gold. But that was hardly possible. The beggar was far in advance in years of this gentleman.

He wanted some flowers, and Iphi was to select them for him to suit her own taste, while he seated himself in the cottage and soon fell into a reverie with his eyes fixed upon the floor, raising his head occasionally and looking off into vacancy.

Iphi and her parents had noticed this strange peculiarity in the beggar. Yet they feared to say so, for they were not certain of his identity. The flowers were selected with great care, and at his request were placed in the chaise.

Iphi returned to the cottage, and the stranger still sat there in meditative silence. At length he said :

" Maiden, here is thy pay," handing her a gold piece.

She attempted to hand him the change but he said, —

" Keep it ; and if you need it not, give it to the poor. I come to this humble abode to ask for favors far more precious than all the gold on earth. I come to this cottage to ask of one whose soul is in accord with Jesus, to save a human soul that is about to be lost. I was led here by the star of Bethlehem. It was such a place where Jesus loved to rest from his toil — where humility and virtue were so eloquent in the sublime praise of the Infinite." The tones of his voice, and the earnest, impressive manner, were the same as the beggar's.

Iphi had now resolved to ask him some questions, with regard to the two sacks of gold, that had been left with them so mysteriously.

He appeared to anticipate her, and quickly said, "Maiden, ask me nothing of the past, my face is turned to

the future. I have a favor to ask of thee, which is beyond
all earthly consideration. Listen! in the palace of Vilani,
there is the Lady Verono, Countess of Vilani. Cruelly
she meditated a deep wrong upon you. I knew it all, and
was ready to save if others had failed. God would not
have allowed the accursed wrong to have gone unpunished.
The time has come, when mercy pleads for her. For now
she is suffering the torments of the lost. I have compassion on her. I want you to ask God to pity and forgive.
I heard her moans, and I thought a human soul had fallen
into the abyss."

Iphi and her parents were moved to tears, at the sad
fate that had fallen on the Lady Verono. They knew
nothing of the cause of this strange statement of her condition. but the deep, earnest, and impressive manner of
this mysterious person, had deeply moved their pity and
compassion.

He arose from his position, and earnestly asked a
blessing on this household ; got into the chaise, and was
driven out into the country, away from the busy city.

V.

WHERE THE GOLD CAME FROM.

THE day following this event, Iphi, while in the city
performing her regular duties, in furnishing her customers
with flowers and fruits, had gathered enough to learn
that the condition of the Countess Vilani, was deplorable.
She heard, also, the result of the trial of Alonzo, and
that Francisco Vilani was still alive, and that he had been
in the habit of appearing in the character of beggar and

hermit. She saw at once, then, that the sacks of gold left
with her, were left by Francisco Vilani, thus disguised as a
beggar, and, that he it was who had on the previous day
bought flowers of her. She had also heard the part that
Alonzo had taken in preserving the life of Francisco, and
had kept him concealed, and away from the power and influence of the late Count Vilani.

She now concluded, further, that Alonzo had been
instrumental in her being released from the power of
Count Vilani, and it further explained to her what Louis
Dejon had said to her before his execution, that he could
not explain anything that took place at the palace, on the
night he had entered it for the purpose of her release, as
all that had been done and said was under the solemn
sanction of an oath. Seeing now the whole matter,
she concluded to go to the palace, and tell Alonzo of the
two sacks of gold that had been left with her, and
describe the person who left them, and also to state that
she believed the person to be Francisco Vilani. When
Iphi returned to the cottage, and related these strange
events to her parents, they were much astonished, and expressed great sympathy for the unfortunate Lady Countess.
Iphi explained to them her intentions of going to Alonzo,
and getting instruction what to do with this gold in their
possession, and they approved of the wisdom of her
course.

Accordingly, she went to the palace, and had an interview with Alonzo. He was sad and mournful, over the
events that had just passed, saying to Iphi that the
Countess Vilani was delirious. That she had several
times sought to take her life with poison, and it required
constant watching to restrain her from self destruction.

Iphi wept, and mentally prayed for the recovery of the unfortunate lady. Alonzo was moved with the charity of this girl, and said to her : " Noble maiden ! Thou art an honor to humanity, thus even to love and forgive thy worst enemies." Iphi answered him by saying she could easily forgive, for she never had hated any human being. She then explained to Alonzo, the event of the beggar leaving with her two sacks of gold, and that since that a person dressed in citizens dress, had come to the cottage and requested her to pray for the Lady Countess, and described as exactly as possible the face and manner of the beggar, and the strange gentleman.

Alonzo then explained to her the history of the two sacks of gold, that Louis had taken them, at his request, to avoid any suspicion from Geno of his real motives in entering the palace on that night; that Louis had concealed the money the next day in the old ruins whence Francisco had taken it, and carried it to the cottage of Iphi.

From some cause, Geno did not get to see Louis, so as to claim from him the money and the keys of the postern gate, and seemed to rest on the good faith of Louis to make it all right with him. On the day following, Geno was arrested for the murder of Vilani, and Louis was with his regiment confined in the garrison, but found some means to communicate to Alonzo the place where he had concealed the money, so that he could at any time recover it. Alonzo explained this whole transaction to Francisco, who at once determined that Iphi should have that gold, to do with it as she deemed best, and that it was the will of God that he should use this gold in this way, so that it might atone for the curse it had brought on others.

Alonzo then told her that the money was the actual property of Francisco ; that he had the undoubted right to give it to whom he pleased ; that it was now her property honestly, justly, and fairly, and to do with it just as she deemed proper and best. That Francisco Vilani would never take it back, nor would he ever allow her to question him on the subject ; and that her mind might be at rest, that he knew the money : he said one sack was fastened with thin wire, while the other was tied with a string.

Iphi was bewildered with the statement of Alonzo. She was as much at loss now how to act, or what to do with so much money, as she was before perplexed about the thought that there was some evil design in thus bestowing upon her so much wealth gratuitously. But time and her natural good sense made this gold atone for the evil it had done in tempting others to the commission of crime.

VI.

REMORSE.

WEEKS and months passed away, and Verono was still confined to her chamber. She required ceaseless care and attention by her attendants. Often in her wild delirium, would she call upon the innocent Iphi to save her, to pity her, and pardon the evil she had done her. When these wild paroxysms of frenzy would pass away, she would fall into a condition of perfect stupor, from which nothing could arouse her to conscious existence. She had the best medical attendants, but nothing could

be done for the unfortunate. A year passed away, and
no change; except an increased physical prostration.
There was this marked trait in her condition, and Alonzo
knew well the cause, that when she did to some extent recover her reason, her mind was so full of appalling reflections, that life was to her a burden, and she wished to
die. For this reason Alonzo wanted to save her life,
believing she might yet be restored to happiness. He
knew all the secrets of her past life, the murder of Vilani,
and the attempt to remove him by a conviction of crime,
and thus silence forever the last witness of her guilt.
Alonzo's life had ever been retired, and without ostentation. Sensible, discreet, and philosophic, he knew that
if this last act of her life was exposed to the public, she
would receive neither charity nor mercy, and be held up to
the vilest contempt and execration. He knew that her
whole life, as a unit, was far more competent to decide
her fate than any angry and misguided public sentiment.

He often times appeared himself as the instrument
of Vilani's cruelty and crime. He preserved his power,
however, to heal the wounds, if he could not save the
victim. He knew that Verono had been betrayed, and had
no sympathy for Vilani, that he had thus fallen a victim
to his own treachery. Had the last act committed by
Verono been exposed, the public would not have known
that Vilani had in fact been the cause of her ruin, and
thus extend to her charity and mercy. It is one of those
cases where the victim suffers the punishment due the
criminal. Sad is it that often times the one who has thus
betrayed an innocent victim, is called a gallant gentleman,
guilty perhaps of a few indiscretions, while the poor victim

of his base passion, is dying in all the agonies of despair, with none to pity, in the dark hours of her misfortune. The unjust decree of public sentiment, without charity, without mercy, condemns the poor victim to the most fearful punishment, while the actual criminal is pardoned, even without the command, "Thou art free, go sin no more."

Alonzo had made the firm and noble resolution to save her life, and with the aid of God to restore her to happiness. He had noticed that oftentimes, when her mind was partially restored, she called on Iphi to pardon her for the wrong she had done. To him this was very hopeful.

Iphi often called at the palace to inquired after the health of the countess. Alonzo in one of these visits, informed her that Verono often called on her to pardon and forgive her.

"My noble benefactor!" exclaimed Iphi, "none but God knows how I would rejoice to save the countess, and restore her to a life of peace and happiness. Myself and my dear parents pray for her restoration. I have nothing to pardon or forgive her for; I never felt towards her any resentment or ill-will."

Alonzo said to her: "I believe if you were present when these intervals of partial restoration of reason occurred, you could save her, and lead her back to life and happiness."

Iphi thought of the generous and noble conduct of Alonzo, in saving Louis from the perilous position, and also in rescuing her from the power of Vilani, and her heart was moved with gratitude, and she replied that there was no earthly comfort or pleasure that she would not forego to restore the Lady Verono to happiness.

Alonzo was the complete master of the entire household. He stated to Iphi that if she would come to the palace and take charge of the countess, and the management of the household, that everything should be at her command. That rooms would be arranged for the reception of her parents, and every comfort supplied them. That he would employ good and faithful gardeners to take care of the cottage, and see to it that everything was kept in order, and with her approval and directions.

This was, in truth, a great sacrifice for her to give up her sweet, pleasant life with her parents in their humble, but loved home. But the appeal was to her generosity, her charity, and mercy, by one who had shown to her all these favors. And after consulting her parents, the arrangement was made, and Iphi, in fact, became the mistress of the palace of Vilani.

Her whole time and attention was devoted to the restoration of Verono. She was constantly by her side, except when she was obliged herself to rest from the weary task. The countess appeared to continue in that same peculiar condition, occasionally waking up as from some terrible dream, and would then act and talk as if she was struggling to escape some horrible doom that threatened her. Iphi at such times was moved with compassion for her, and oftentimes would soothe her to rest with tender words.

She managed with the most exact economy and care. The servants of the entire establishment, respected and loved their new mistress, and having a good example set before them, they also became attentive, careful, and industrious. The dishonest Joseph, who had been one of Geno's tools and confederates in crime, was given to understand by Alonzo, that he had detected him in his crime in stealing the gold referred to; Joseph plead so earnestly for pardon, that Alonzo told him he would now watch him closely, and if he detected in him the last act of villiany, would hand him over to the officers of the law for punishment.

Iphi's parents led a quiet, retired life, but it was not the pleasant cottage life they had been used to, but their beloved child was following in the course of duty, and they really felt happy in making this sacrifice to please her.

The shadows of evil that had clung to this palace of Vilani, had passed away to a great extent, and if Iphi, in her mission of love and care for the unfortunate countess, should be successful in restoring her to life, one of the greatest desires would be accomplished. When the countess would lay in apparent death-like stupor, and then arouse to consciousness, she was so miserable and hopeless, that poor Iphi almost despaired. At such times the strange, weird image of Francisco, when last she saw him, would rise up before her, pleading in his impressive manner, to save a soul that was about to fall in the dark abyss, to cling in mercy to the unfortunate Verono. She was nerved to stand fast in this mission of love that demanded her charity and mercy.

The countess had mocked her faith ; yet, she loved her none the less, for she pitied her unbelief. The countess had, with the most unfeeling cruelty, trampled upon the dearest feelings of her heart, used her as a base instrument to perpetrate crime and iniquity. Yet she never felt for her the least resentment for these wrongs, but would say, " How sorrowful to think that God has forsaken this

lost one. Oh, how I would rejoice if he would save her,
and restore her to a life of peace and happiness!"

VII.

THE GOOD ANGEL.

THE sun arose in splendor from the waves of its ocean
bed. Soon, and the glad waters and the smiling landscape, were basking in the radiant glory of an Italian
morn. The air was laden with the sweet perfume of
the orange blossom, the blossom of the purple vine, and
the blooming flowers. The sequestered and perfumed
shadows of the orange and citron groves were filled with
the sweet melody of birds. The busy hum of commerce
came up from the shore, the market-place, and the thronged
streets. It was the freshness and vigor of morning life.
The palace of Vilani was wrapt in gloom, for the shadows
of death fell upon its portals. He did not enter, for God
had decreed life; the prayers of Iphi had reached the
mercy seat.

Iphi, sat watching with intense interest, every change
or motion of the Countess De Vilani. True to her noble
nature, she would rejoice greatly over the salvation of the
one that was supposed to be lost. It was like that tender,
holy love, of the fond mother, over the wayward, apostate
son. The love is great, for pity and compassion melts the
heart into extreme tenderness. The countess sighed, and
attracted Iphi's attention. The classic features of Verono
in former days so marked with majestic beauty, so commanding and attractive, were now expressive of a plain-

tive, thoughtful sadness. She spoke to Iphi in an audible tone. Iphi looked at her with amazement; the look of terror that had often been partially veiled by the radiant beauty of Verono, had disappeared, and left a smile that was full of faith and love. Iphi mentally asked herself, "Oh, can it be possible, that heaven has blessed my prayers, and realized my fond hopes?"

The countess said to her, "My dear Iphi, you have come to me at last. You are the good angel to bring me pardon. How my poor heart has longed for this hour, when Iphi would come and drive away the specter of despair. Blessed maiden, I have found out in my dreams, that the worship of Isis and Jupiter were but the brilliant images of fancy, and things of earth and time. But the Faith, Charity, and Mercy of Jesus connects the soul with the Infinite, who is supreme over all things of time and eternity. God has sent you to me, dear maiden, with pardon and love."

"Dear Lady! I have never ceased to love you. I have been with you long; and have ever prayed, and fondly hoped for the coming of this blessed hour. I have not the power to pardon; but how thankful I am that God has pardoned you." She pressed the lips of the countess with the kiss of love, while her tears of holy joy fell upon the pale, wan cheek, so marked with long suffering.

The arms of the once proud, lofty, ambitious Countess De Vilani clasped to her embrace the Flower Girl, who had said to her in days past, the religion of Jesus is imperishable, for it teaches us Love, Charity, and Mercy. She clings to Iphi, as if her only salvation was to anchor to this grand being, who was now to her the only link between time and eternity. They were alone in this apartment, in this peaceful, happy morning hour. The shadows of death, in search of a victim, no longer fell upon the portals of the palace. And, doubtless, this Greek maiden, with the genius of her race and the inspiration of the hour, heard the angels, song and felt the presence of Infinite love.

VIII.

FRANCISCO AND CALVETTI.

"WHAT has become of Francisco?" was often asked by Alonzo and Iphi. Neither he nor his attendant had been heard from for many months. Alonzo now became alarmed, and regretted that he had not paid more attention of late to his movements. He had every confidence in the integrity and good sense of the person he had placed in charge. They had both left the house occupied by them, and the chaise was there; but the horse had been left in the care of one of the neighbors, with instructions to keep him until their return.

What most astonished Alonzo, was that the attendant did not inform him of his departure, but he at length concluded that it was some fancy that had seized Francisco, that no one except himself and his attendant knew what he was doing. There was no person in Leghorn who had ever seen him to know him since he left the Hall of Justice, on the day of Alonzo's trial. He had been seen by rumor, for every beggar who was unknown, or pilgrim, or trading pedler, was declared to be the insane count, appearing in different places at the same time.

Alonzo's anxiety was at length relieved by receiving a letter from Calvetti, Francisco's attendant, informing him that Francisco had taken a notion to go to Palestine, and the Holy Land, and that when they left Leghorn, Francisco had commanded him in the strongest terms, to inform no one of his departure; he left in the character and dress of a pilgrim; Calvetti took means enough to defray expenses; that he had taken good care of him, and watched over him carefully, and that nothing had occurred to interrupt them in their travels.

Francisco had given as a reason that he could not remain satisfied at Leghorn, and if his plans had been known, some one would interfere with his designs. Francisco was content, as he had left Verono in the hands of Iphi, that no evil could befall the good Alonzo, and that he was now writing to him with Francisco's consent. He further stated that in one of the ports of the Mediterranean they had fallen in with an American merchant vessel called the "Lafayette," commanded by a captain of the name of Smith, and that Francisco was much charmed with his description of the Great Republic, where the people ruled and had no king. This Captain Smith was almost as strange and eccentric to me as my ward! Francisco. He would often say to me : "Calvetti ! by Moses, this man of yours has more good sense mixed up with his insanity than any madman I have ever seen in my born days."

"This sea-captain was so much taken with Francisco's strange manner that he was exceedingly anxious to learn his history; but, of course, Francisco would have forbidden me giving it to him. He was satisfied, however, with me telling him he was a nobleman who was supposed to be insane; but the few persons who knew him well, believed that it was nothing more than a great degree of eccentricity, and that he was under the influence of a wild ungovernable fancy that he must act for the happiness and benefit of the human race; that he possessed a noble, generous heart, but visionary in the practical application of his good intentions.

" Francisco's attachment to Captain Smith daily increased, so that, at length, nothing could induce him, when he arrived at Leghorn, to quit the vessel and return home, and rest for a time. Captain Smith assured me, that if he insisted on staying with him, he would be amply protected and cared for, and that everything he could do to make him comfortable and contented would be done. Francisco insisted on me going ashore and arranging for funds necessary to pay expenses to the United States and return, with the further injunction that I was not to make it known to any one where he was going." This letter to Alonzo was dated at Marseilles, and written on their way to see the Grand Republic that Captain Smith had described in such glowing terms.

Alonzo was satisfied with this account, for he was well convinced that nothing could be done to change his intentions, and that if he was to use force or violence on Francisco to keep him confined, and deprive him of self-reliance and liberty, it would have a very bad effect on his mind, and perhaps reproduce absolute insanity; and there was that strange fancy, that seemed to have entire possession of him, that he wanted no one to know who he was.

BOOK XII.

ANNETTA.

I.

MURAT.

Murat, King of Naples, maintained his power by clemency, even after Napoleon's downfall and imprisonment on the Island of Elba. But when the Emperor had escaped, and again returned to France, Murat, in his effort to assist him to regain his lost power, was betrayed by pretended friends into the hands of his enemies; and on the 19th of October, A. D. 1815, he was put to death by the order of Ferdinand.

What greater praise is there for the memory of the dead than to say he was brave among the bravest; that he was a hero, confronting in battle the heroic; that his heart was moved to pity and compassion for every human being that was stricken with sorrow; that he was merciful even to the merciless? Splendid as were his achievements as a commander, they were surpassed by the grandeur of his magnanimity, his kindness, his charity.

II.

Years have passed away — years that have been marked with the most marvellous events in the history of Europe.

Napoleon has escaped from Elba, and is again preparing for that final contest on the bloody field of Waterloo. The historian has well described these grand historical events; we have a more humble theme, by taking the Alps valley, the birthplace of Paul Lorraine, and speaking to you of the virtues of the humble and good. It has changed but little since we last saw it. Paul is still there, in the memory of the hearts who loved him so well. There is the boy — now almost a man — that he grasped from the jaws of death on the verge of the abyss. He loves to tell people how good Paul Lorraine was. The little children who followed him with sadness and sorrow when first he left for the battle-field, now grown up to be men and women, talk with touching pathos of their dear Paul who had gone from them, never to return. There is still the grand old mountains, the forest, the fields, the brook, and the cemetery where the beloved dead repose in their lonely graves. There is still the Lorraine cottage; the good old mother and Annetta. There, too, is the cottage where Annetta was born and where her parents died; and there is still that vine-covered porch from which Paul and Annetta oftentimes watched the stars and selected one for their abiding-place in the immortal world. Uncle Louis now had charge of this property, and, with the aid of his two sons, had spare time to assist Annetta and the good mother in the care of their place. It was still a beautiful happy home; yet there are many things to remind them of their sad bereavement.

Annetta has oftentimes thought of what she had said to Paul, "If you were to die, I feel as if I could not live. I would not grieve and mourn uselessly; but I would feel as if severed from earth, and like the vine severed from its root, fade, wither, and perish." She oftentimes thought that if it was not for her old mother and uncle Louis, she would gladly go to the star Paul and herself had chosen as their abiding-place in the other world. Although Paul had died the death of a condemned man, the generous Murat, in his last letter of condolence to them, declared that it was a noble, heroic sacrifice, to save the armies of his country from demoralization; that it was a voluntary offer to save the lives of others, equally, if not more to blame for the unfortunate calamity than he; that he was betrayed into it through his noble conduct in rescuing an innocent girl from a most cruel fate. Annetta had heard detailed the generous conduct of Paul in rescuing Iphi, and her heart rejoiced in the brave and noble conduct of her dear Paul. When she looked out upon the lofty cliffs of the Alps, and, in memory, saw him pass along on their craggy heights, with eyes dimmed with tears she would exclaim, "Oh! he was so good — so true and kind to all — surely God will take care of so good a one."

Mother Lorraine was greatly consoled with the statement of Murat, that his death was in honor; not dishonor. She saw that this act did not involve any criminal intent, and that God would pardon him for this, when his whole life was so full of love and kindness for others.

III.

Uncle Louis Lorraine was still, and had ever been, the true and faithful friend of the good old mother and Annetta. One day Louis received a letter. It had been postmarked at Marseilles. He opened it and it read as follows: —

"Dear Uncle Louis, — I am still living. Oh! my dear mother! my dear Annetta! How my poor heart longs to embrace them. I have thus written to you, so that you might, with your good sense and discretion, gradually convey to them this intelligence. I would have written this to you long since, but I was fearful that I might in some way compromise the position of my dear preserver with the Emperor Napoleon; and I would suffer death gladly before that should occur. Even yet, Uncle Louis, you need not make this public. You will, in a short time, receive word to be at Marseilles at a certain time, where arrangements have been made to have you all come to me —mother, Annetta, yourself and sons. Tell mother and Annetta to keep strong, so that they can endure a long journey. God has been good to me, and he will yet allow me to see once more on earth the beloved ones of my heart. In love. Paul Lorraine."

Louis sat down and wept tears of joy. Could it be possible that God, in His infinite goodness, would again permit them once more on earth to clasp to their hearts the happy, good, brave boy, that left them so many years ago, and whose death they had mourned so many sorrowful days and nights. Louis saw that his task was one of difficulty. He had to converse with mother and Annetta about Paul, and at the same time conceal his feelings, when his heart was full. It was about the usual hour for him to visit the cottage, and he concluded to go at once and commence on the subject by degrees. Annetta had endured so many sorrows— the death of her parents, her infant, and her husband, — that it had marked her pale face with sadness, and given a touching, plaintive tone to her voice.

Louis commenced forthwith, and said that he sometimes thought he would yet see Paul.

Annetta said, "Since I have looked at you, Uncle Louis, you look a great deal more cheerful than common, what does it all mean uncle? tell us; do, pray?"

"I was thinking over a certain clause in the letter which the king of Naples wrote you first, and I am now convinced that he intended it for a hope. He said, 'Do not sorrow too much, for in the end it will be well.' What did he mean, in the end it will be well? Well, in this world, or in the world to come?"

"Oh, Uncle Louis! do not say anything that would give us hope, without any possibility that it will be true! The disappointment would be so hard for me to bear."

"No, no, Annetta! God forbid that I should trifle with your feelings, but I have often thought much about this matter, and I tell you Annetta, that I do believe that Paul is still living."

"Oh, Uncle Louis! I do not know what to think of your strange words, and you cannot conceal a joyful look on your face, that has not been there for a long time. And I am not able to tell why it is so."

Uncle Louis addressed himself to the mother, to procure him Murat's letter, informing her the first time of the sad fate of her son. The letter was procured, and the sentence was as Louis had said, "Do not sorrow too much for him, for in the end all will be well."

"Annetta, now listen to me. The king of Naples was ordered to execute every man in the regiment who had participated in the mutiny. Murat, of his own accord, mitigated the positive command of the emperor, in agreeing to accept three who should suffer death as an example to others. Paul was not chosen by lot, but volunteered to suffer for the balance, so also did his noble, brave companions. This very act had moved Murat with such admiration of the heroic conduct of Paul, Jean, and Louis, and knowing too, at this time, the generous part they had taken in the rescue of Iphi, that he resolved at all hazards to save their lives, and have the emperor believe he had executed his order. If it was believed by the whole entire army, that they had suffered death for the offence, the example to deter others was thus accomplished. Paul could not risk even writing to his relatives or friends, for fear of compromising his noble, generous preserver. And thus it is, my dear Annetta, and dear mother, that I believe that our beloved boy is yet alive."

The good old mother sat silent. Her heart was full of prayer and thankfulness. To her it was apparent that God had put it in the heart of this grand man to be merciful to her dear son, and save his life. Her heart was convinced that she would yet see her darling boy, and with tears of joy dimming her aged eyes, she thanked the Infinite goodness that had spared his life.

Annetta's heart was almost bursting with emotion. She said, "Oh, dear Uncle Louis! can it be, can it be, that our dear, dear Paul is yet alive? I always thought he was so good, true, and brave, that every one would be merciful to him and save him from evil, and that the good angel would guard him. Oh! Uncle Louis! is Paul still alive? Can it be? can it be, that the dear one yet lives?"

Louis saw that her emotion was intense, and he said to her, "Dear Annetta, calm yourself. Excessive joy is quite as dangerous as excessive grief. If Paul is alive, it will require all your fortitude and strength to go to him, for he is far away. Would it not be better for me to call again, and we will talk this matter over when you have become more composed."

"Dear Uncle Louis, I know what your kindness means. You know something that you have not yet told us. I have more fortitude, more strength, than you think I have, Uncle Louis. I could travel to the utmost parts of the earth, to see my beloved. God will give me strength to go to him, be he where he may. Were you to leave me now, I could not rest, with the belief that you had some knowledge of our dear one, that you have feared to tell us, and my anxiety would be too fearful to bear."

Louis saw the force of Annetta's remark, and for a while was silent and thoughtful. Annetta had thus far showed a strength and fortitude that he never dreamed she possessed. He looked upon her pale, thin face, and saw at a glance that there was a will and resolution that amazed him.

No one can properly estimate in others, the power and grandeur of this firm reliance on the love, charity, and mercy, of a supreme being. We know nothing of the power of this faith on the hearts of others. They cannot themselves explain this wonderful conviction of feeling, that nothing can change or weaken. It was this faith that Louis could not see or appreciate, and this was the source of the strength of Annetta, that to him was marvellous. He therefore drew from his pocket the letter, and deliberately and slowly read it to Annetta and Mother Lorraine. Annetta, without saying a word, took it and read it, then kissed it, and bathed the precious letter with a flood of tears. Each one was silently returning thanks

UNCLE LOUIS READING PAUL'S LETTER TO ANNETTA AND
MOTHER LORRAINE. Page 190.

to God, and the merciful king, who had been so good to their son, and charitable to them all.

It was that kind of pure, exalted, and holy gratitude, that was acceptable to heaven. How the kind heart of the merciful king would have rejoiced in the sweet incense of this praise offered up to him from the souls of these humble peasants. The grandeur of his victory, on the field of Jena, was nothing against the sublime act of mercy that saved the lives of these heroic sons of France. Man praised the victory of Jena, but God blessed him for his charity and mercy.

IV.

RELIGION AND GOVERNMENT.

We have not the desire to assail any creed or theology. They are taught in the schools, and are, to a great extent, known best to the learned and educated. But faith in the existence of a supreme intelligence, hope for immortality, and charity for mankind, are attributes of the human soul, that, in the words of the atheist, have been evolved by the operation of cause and effect.

They are not produced by education, but are improved and enlightened by education, and sad is it they are often perverted by the same cause.

Every human soul has been moved with faith in a power above man and earth. Every human soul has been gladened with hope. Every human heart has been touched with love and sympathy.

It is this that has made the teachings of Jesus of Nazareth imperishable. Primitive Christianity will survive all creeds, all theology, all the doctrines and teachings of the schools.

Shakespeare and Burns awakened these feelings in the human heart, touched that tender cord of union and sympathy in the human breast, and made their names immortal. They are not only admired, but they are loved.

We do not see God with physical or mental eye. We do not reason ourselves into the belief of his existence. We do not believe in his existence on account of miracles performed. It is the genius of the heart that makes us feel, rather than the mind to think, that there is, over and above all, a supreme intelligence, whose wisdom is far beyond our finite comprehension. There have been men of that cast of genius, that they feel great truths rather than see them. Robert Burns, with his grand heart, with its force and power, made millions of human beings feel great truths, with greater force than reason or logic could have done. He felt great truths to exist, and he made others feel their force and beauty, so impressive, that they never forget them. The human heart feels, outside of revelation or miracles, that there is a supreme intelligence above man. Martyrs who have died for their faith, or have fallen in the cause of human liberty, died believing that they were in harmony with the Infinite. Robert Emmet, the grandest example of martyrdom, in the cause of liberty, in the history of man, felt in his last hour that God was present with him. Not that he was with him in a personal sense, but his soul was in accord with the divine attributes of the Infinite.

The human heart cannot rest satisfied with the belief,

that in all these vast realms, countless, endless, unnumbered worlds, that man on this little earth is the only being that thinks, knows, or feels. The astronomer, by figures, facts, and logic, tells us that there are in the heavens shining stars whose light is thousands of years traversing the space between them and earth. And they are no nearer the end of creation than we, for there is no end. The atheist tells us that man is evolved, by cause and effect, from the very lowest order of creation. The atheist who stands in his lofty tower, with his wide, expansive horizon for his view, and can see no God, is himself a god of the first magnitude, and looks with scorn upon both Moses and Jesus, while the grand army of love and charity, who go with man in the dreary walks of his pilgrimage on earth, to cheer him in his sorrows, bring joy to hearts in despair, teach him Faith, Hope and Charity, are but little pigmies, groping in darkness, for they cannot see the light. Every Pagan martyr had hopes of immortality, when he perished for his faith. Every Jewish martyr died in the firm belief that there was a God who would reward his sufferings. Every Christian martyr felt in the hour of his death, the inspiration of immortal joy. Socrates, whose life was said to be pure and good, was willing to die rather than live, denying the existence of one supreme being who was above all things of time and eternity.

The splendor of the orations of Demosthenes and Cicero, are enduring monuments of the grand inspiration of genius. But the Sermon on the Mount is above them all, for it was inspired with the love, charity, and mercy of the Infinite.

Infidelity of this period is uncharitable, for the church of the fourteenth century is not the church of the nineteenth century. The bigotry of this present period is not so dangerous to the downfall of liberty as the bitter, uncharitable partisan, who would sacrifice country for party, and would sooner gain a political triumph, than to secure liberty and establish justice.

History proves another thing that infidelity will not admit. In all ages, while bigotry and intolerance were cursing the world with unnumbered, countless acts of cruelty, Christian charity went forth in its mission of love to heal the wounds made by this ruthless hate. With the tender touch of loving hands it has cooled the fevered brow of the dying Pagan, Christian, Jew. It has kissed the tears from the cheek of dying Infidel — for Jesus said, "love even thine enemies." In the last hours loving lips have whispered words of hope and consolation. Thanks to this grand army of charity that have so blessed suffering humanity in all ages. Thanks to these noble souls who have so often, with tears of pity, moistened the pillow of the death-bed of friend and foe.

The bigot, or the hypocrite, has not one-half the power to destroy liberty and the rights of man in the nineteenth century, as the demogogue or the unjust partisan, who slanders his opponents on the one side and, with infamous hypocrisy, conceals the villany of his own partisans. In truth, since our Fathers so wisely divorced church and state, there is no danger of a subversion of the state by the church, but there can be no constitutional barrier against the demagogue, if he can, with his eloquence, deceive and betray the people to ruin.

The love of liberty is natural in the human heart. The

demogogue opens the pathway for the ambition of the despot. Bigotry and intolerance produce the infidel and the atheist. The first are the silent, unseen assassins of faith, hope, and charity, while the latter are the open and armed enemies of all religion. They are both dogmatic, presumptuous, intolerant and void of charity. They carry in their pockets rules to measure other men's intelligence. The bigot has a narrow creed or theology to judge men's faith in a religion that is infinite in its magnanimity and grandeur. The infidel measures all by a materialistic view, and all that do not come up to his standard, are fools or knaves; and thus, they both are waging relentless war on faith, hope, and charity.

The political partisan, actuated by ambition, is the deadly foe of liberty.

The bigot and the intolerant are the deadly enemies of faith, hope, and charity.

We do not love liberty less, we do not love faith, hope, and charity less, but we love them more, for they have been betrayed by their pretended friends.

Bigotry and intolerance, void of charity, with their narrow creeds, have filled the world with woe. Their pathways have been marked in all ages, with agony and tears. Often has Christianity been assassinated in the house of its friends, and thus put arguments in the mouths of its open enemies to destroy its virtues. Had it not been so, long centuries back, faith, hope, and charity, would have blessed the nations of the earth.

The great mind of Napoleon gave utterance in substance to this thought. Alexander, Hannibal, and Cæsar conquered empires, and were renowned in antiquity, and their names have survived the centuries. Jesus is above them all, with a life of perfect humility. He is remembered for his love of mankind; surely he was more than mortal. Here then Napoleon struck the living, vital principal that is imperishable, and will survive as long as human heart throbs in human breast.

It is the faith, hope, and charity, offered to man in his dreary pilgrimage on **earth.**

BOOK XIII.

I.

THE EXILES.

NAPOLEON is imprisoned on the Island of St. Helena. Mysterious destiny. Are the marvellous triumphs of this peerless man to close forever? Such was the decree of the Supreme will. Why this was so we know not, the Infinite mind alone knows. Perhaps he had violated some supreme law of justice, for which there was no pardon. Perhaps there was a period in his strange, wonderful life, when destiny gave him the power to choose between good and evil, and said to him, here are two roads in thy life, choose for thyself.

The one is Josephine, and the love of the people, Marengo, Jena, Austerlitz, Victory, Liberty, Republic for France, and the doctrine of self-government, secured to his country forever, the love and praise of mankind, the approval of divine justice, with a triumph unsurpassed in history.

The other was divorce from Josephine, and wed the queenly Louisa, and get a throne among the kings, furnish France with a line of kings; betrayed and imprisoned on the Island of Elba, escape, again betrayed on the field of Waterloo, again exiled on the Island of St. Helena, to die in despair.

When he divorced Josephine perhaps he divorced his good angel as well as the hearts of the people. Who knows? God knows.

II.

LOUISIANA.

In the fore part of this century there were two Frenchmen, by the name of Harrold who purchased and moved into a small plantation not very far from the city of New Orleans.

They were represented as brothers. The younger one was named Francis Harrold, the elder one Claude. Francis was very lively and cheerful, while Claude was much more thoughtful, and at times looked and acted as if some sad and sorrowful memory was resting upon his heart.

He was very reserved, and had but little communication with his neighbors, and in fact, never, without he was engaged in performing some act of charity or friendship.

There were many of their friends who made inquiries with regard to Claude, that did not arise from mere selfish curiosity. They did not think that this man was sad from remorse, or conscious guilt.

They would say this : " He is a good man, I am sure of that. I would like to know why he is so sad at times, for perhaps it is in my power to assist him, which I would like so much to do."

He was very industrious, worked hard, both himself and Francis. They lived well and comfortably. The plantation was small, and everything was in order and looked neat and tidy. The house was a one story cottage, with four rooms on the first floor, and with one or two sleeping rooms in the other story formed by the high peaked French gables. Back of the house, there was a long line of high, dense forests of oak, cyprus, and walnut, interspersed with magnolia. It rose up clear cut from the cultivated fields, and at the dim twilight hour looked like an army of mighty giants standing as sentinels over this happy home.

The interior of the house was plain, neat, and comfortable, in its outfit. The walls were decorated with French lithographs of scenes in France. In one of the rooms there was an oil painting of great excellence as a work of art. It was the picture of a French officer on horseback, dashing along on the shore of a sea. In the back ground was a perfect representation of a volcano, sending forth its lurid flames.

The person represented was no ordinary personage. His appearance was peculiarly impressive. And the lights and shadows of the burning volcano gave the whole work a cast of gloomy grandeur.

They made frequent visits to New Orleans to see their friend, Pierre Lavasse, and a very special kind one he had been to the brothers, both Francis and Claude.

The city of New Orleans was very much indebted for her great prosperity to the enterprising Frenchmen who had emigrated there. Every commercial city of France had its representatives in all the departments of commerce and industry.

Our friend, Pierre Lavasse, referred to in a former chapter, and the friend of Captain Smith, had been instrumental in procuring this plantation for the brothers Harrold, and had also sold them a negro boy, called Tom, who was of great value to them every way.

When the neighbors failed to draw from either Claude or Francis Harrold where they came from, and some clue to their former history, they commenced to question Tom on the subject.

Tom would say, "I cum from New Orleans, sar, and dar I fus met massa Harrold. He axed me, 'Tom, you go wid me to plantation?' I look at him face, and I says, 'Yes, massa, Tom go wid you sure.'"

When they asked Tom where he came from, he gave them all the information on that subject desired.

"I cum from New Orleans, sar; been raised dar. Belong to massa Pierre Lavasse. One day, dis long ago, massa Pierre, he say to me, 'Tom, you be one good boy, by jingo, and he say, I want to sell you Tom, but I no sell you 'cept you want to go wid de man what want you, Tom.' Den I say, 'Who am de man, massa Pierre?' Den he say, 'massa Harrold am de man.' Well, den I says, 'massa, him all right. I go wid massa Harrold.' So you see Tom am here."

Tom lived here with perfect equality, as far as comforts of life were concerned. His yoke was easy, and his burdens light, but no man knows so well how the human soul longs to be released from bondage, as he who has been enslaved. And how the heart throbs when he sees the dawn of his emancipation. And no one knows the joys of liberty, so well as the heart that has felt the warmth of its generous flame.

If Tom had even been emancipated by his master Harrold, he would not have left him. There were thousands of negroes who fled from comfortable homes and kind masters, far away into the cold, cheerless climate of Canada, and thus rent asunder the dearest ties that cling to the human heart, the love of home. And when far, far away, their hearts were ever turning to that dear place where the old folks stay. You may think it strange they should leave when well treated, and loved their homes; the place of their birth, with all of this attachment, so very strong and natural with the negro. The cause was mainly owing to the dreadful fate that hangs over every human being in bondage.

When I say that a love of home, kindred, and friends, is natural with the negro, I mean to be understood as asserting that no people in this world are more strongly attached to the place of their birth, or have more love, attachment, and gratitude, for those who treat them kindly, than the negro race.

The French people, as a class, were not hard task-masters, when you compare them with the emigrants from the Northern States, in the South.

It was generally conceded, that emigrants from the Northern States were more exacting, and cruel, with their slaves, as a class, than the native-born slaveholder.

But it is a joyful thing that legalized bondage no longer exists in any State in the Union. Glad, and full of thanks, should we be that it is ended, and we hope forever.

The price paid for this emancipation, however, was great. It has left sad and mournful memories in thousands of once happy-homes, North and South. The money and time wasted and thrown away, was nothing in the balance, against the lives of thousands of noble, heroic men, who fell on the battle-fields.

They were all our countrymen, both North and South. Noble hearts, that had throbbed in unison, at the very name of Bunker Hill, fell in battle as foes; engaged the one against the other, in deadly strife. It was brother slaying brother. Countrymen against countrymen. It was the horrible, ghastly picture of national suicide.

It is vain and idle to talk about who was to blame for this calamity.

The North exercised no degree of charity towards the South, and the South became frenzied with passion, and rushed madly to their destruction.

The demagogues, both North and South, actuated by ambition, absolutely seized these wild passions of the people for selfish purposes, and led them into war, and disunion.

There never was a time when, if the North and South had have acted together in a patriotic and charitable spirit, and taken the advice of such men as Clay, Webster, Lincoln, and Douglass, the Union could not have been preserved in peace, and the gradual emancipation of the negro secured in the end.

I say Lincoln, because he never was in favor, in principle, of any other mode of emancipation, except gradual emancipation on the basis of peace. No man ever heard him utter any opinions or sentiments that were calculated in any way to arouse the passions of hate, or enmity, against any section of the country.

And yet it is passing strange that even at this day you will find men of great and commanding talents, for base and selfish purposes, still striving to keep alive the fires of hate, malice, and revenge. And some of them think that reconciliation, charity, and patriotic forbearance, and peace, are of far less consequence than securing the spoils of office, by a party triumph.

It would be far better to inform the people of this country what were the mistakes made that produced this terrible loss of life. What were the mistakes made that have postponed peace and reconciliation, and have preserved the Union, only in name, with a cold, lifeless form, void of heart and soul.

In future times, the uncharitable dealers in vituperation, North and South, will be regarded as the disturbers of the public peace. And though, perhaps not always designedly, they were, in fact and in truth, acting as absolute enemies to the peace and prosperity of the Union.

III.

THE war of 1812 with England is over. The conflict was short and decisive. The victory of Andrew Jackson, over Packingham, here at New Orleans, was one of the grandest achievements in our history. The naval engagements were marked, on the part of the Yankee sailor, with a heroism unsurpassed.

Captain Ethan Allen Smith had done what he said he would. He placed his gallant ship, the Lafayette, on a war footing; received some iron dogs from the government; took Charley Convors as first lieutenant; entered the service, and struck many a valiant blow on the side of justice and liberty. The war over, the Lafayette is again engaged in legitimate commerce.

Our good old friend, Pierre Lavasse, is still in New Orleans, the same honest, sincere, open-hearted Frenchman, as when first we saw him on board the Lafayette, greeting his friend, Captain Ethan Smith, on his return from the Mediterranean. They still indulged a little in their bumpers, by the way of toasts to the respective flags of the United States and France. On their first meeting and last parting, they were not, however, intemperate in their habits. Madame Lavasse was still the kind, amiable wife, mother, and friend, still presiding, with graceful dignity, over the old-fashioned mansion of Pierre Lavasse.

On one occasion, when Pierre met Captain Smith, he said to him, "I tell you Captain Smit, you'r best judge of a man in dese United States sure, by jingo."

"I really believe you'r right, Pierre. When I see a man sailing over the waters, I can tell if he will answer the helm of duty, and come up square to the work laid out for him to do. Let us take a small drink to the health of these Exiles I have brought over the waters to this land of liberty."

"I will drink to that toast sure, my best friend, Captain Smit. But let me tell you how you be good judge of man. Good many years ago, before ze war, I ask you to get me good clerk."

"Well, Pierre, did I not get him for you?"

"Yes, by jingo; listen! You git me good clerk. You git de United States good soldier. You git Pierre Lavasse good partner. You git my dear daughter Eva a good husband. By jingo, Captain Smit, Charley Convors good for everytings; best boy in dis town."

"I knew it when I recommended him. And Charley and Eva are married, Pierre; well done, God bless them, Pierre! And now, Pierre, the only thing I regret is, that I was not present at this marriage. But Mrs. Lavasse, Caroline, Charley, and Eva, are all well, are they?"

"All well, Captain Smit, very happy, and all looking anxious for our old friend, Captain Smit!"

"Well, Pierre, we must drink the health of Charley and Eva, for it is the best news I have heard for some time."

"We feel indebted to our good friend, the captain, for this, and I send the boy and carriage down to the ship for you to come to mansion and stay with us as usual."

"Thank you, Pierre; thank you. I will avail myself of the great pleasure of spending a large portion of my time with your amiable and happy family."

IV.

FRANCISCO.

IT is now far advanced in the year 1816. Claude Harrold is still living on his little plantation, where everything is cheerful and blooming with industry, economy, and thrift. The faithful Tom is still with him, and strongly attached to his benevolent master. Francis is no longer with him, and he has in his place his mother and wife. The neighbors no longer ask the question, "Why is such a good man so often sad and sorrowful?"

They say now, that it is strange he should have lived so long without them, and as this subject is never introduced by Claude himself, it has passed away with the years that have gone.

What had become of Francis, was a question that was often asked. This question was generally answered by the knowing ones in this way: —

"About a year ago there came to the city of New Orleans, with Captain Smith, a strange looking Italian nobleman, whose general appearance indicated either insanity, or a remarkable degree of eccentricity of character. He had with him an intelligent, smart man, who acted as secretary, companion, and servant. There was no lack of money, and he had a perfect passion for doing deeds of kindness and charity. No one knew his name, and he was designated as the strange Italian count. The name of his companion was Calvetti. They were well acquainted with Pierre Lavasse, and Charley Convors, and Claude Harrold. It was stated that when this strange Italian count left the city of New Orleans on the Lafayette, commanded by Captain Smith, Francis, Claude's brother, went with them on the same vessel, but where he or the count went, no one knew, or by the most diligent curiosity could ever find out."

Questions were sometimes asked Claude where his brother had gone, and he answered by saying that Francis was a young man, and had gone out into the world to seek his fortune.

There were no great changes made in this pleasant home as to style or adornment. Everything was neat, tidy, and had a happy look.

As to inmates, the change was remarkable. An elderly lady, with a pleasant, neat appearance was there, represented as the mother of Claude and Francis.

There was also a middle-aged lady, with a sweet, plaintive smile on her face, said to be the wife of Claude Harrold. The joy of the mother and wife appeared to be in their love and devotion to Claude.

Negro Tom was delighted with his old missus, and the young missus. This sable son of Africa, stood ready at all times, with the gratitude of his race, to do or to make any sacrifice for their comfort and happiness. Tom was often sent to New Orleans for supplies for the house, and he never failed to go to the Pierre Lavasse mansion, to see his good old masser and missus.

The lives of those who dwell in this cottage was like a long summer day, full of joy and sunlight, with perfect peace. Nothing occurred to disturb this serene and quiet mode of life, until about the year 1825 or '26.

Well on towards night-fall, Tom came into the cottage all excitement and alarm. The white of his expanded eyelids gave him a look of terror.

"Mass Claude," he said, "I believe de harry cane is comin', sure."

"Why do you think so, Tom," said Claude.

"I tell you, massa, de sea am gone up in the sky, and de sky am green as the sea. De sun am gone away behind de big green sky, der am no black clouds massa, and it am so berry still you can hear a pin drop. By and by you hear him roar ober in de woods yonder; den he bery soon bust up eberyting. Down come de cotton, de corn, and de big trees, and maybe de house. Hope not massa. Listen massa, hear him comin'."

Claude looked at the sky, and as Tom said, the sky had the strange, peculiar tint and appearance of the ocean at rest, with a deep, blue, greenish cast. The setting sun was concealed, not in the usual appearance of a clouded sky, with the storm outlined; but the whole sky was covered with this peculiar tint.

He listened, and as Tom had said, he heard distinctly over the woods, and off in the west a moaning sound, that was evidently growing louder, and drawing nearer.

A frightened deer came out of the forest, pursued by the huntsman's eager hounds; passed through the field, and fled towards the distant bayou; and night and darkness came, and with them the howling tempest. It was as if the demon of the air had let loose his armed myrmidons commanding them to destroy and desolate the earth. The angry winds swept the fields, destroyed the promise of harvest, and dashed to the earth at times the majestic forest trees. The rain fell in torrents. The thunder rolled, and the lightning's lurid flash blazed athwart the sky.

Hark! a cry for help! Ah, Claude Harrold, little do you at this moment dream of the loved one, who, amidst this beating storm, calls on you for help! Never, never in your life will you forget that cry for help! Little do you dream that for the one who cries "Save me, or I perish!" you would gladly quit fortune, life, and everything on earth, but honor, to save him from death. The quick discernment of the slave Tom was the first to hear, even above the roar of the wild storm, that agonizing cry for help. And little did he think that from that moment destiny had decreed, that the chains of bondage had fallen from his limbs, and that no man on earth could call him slave again.

It was the hour of his emancipation. He says, "Masser Harrold, I hear some one out yonder towards de wood cry for help."

"Is it possible, Tom, that any poor unfortunate can be out in such a tempest?"

He listened, and above the noise of the fearful storm, he heard a wailing cry for help. Claude had by accident set a light in the window looking out towards the forest, and the lost stranger who cried for help, had been long and bravely trying to reach this light in the window, to him so full of hope in this hour of peril.

Claude looked out of the window, and when the flash of lightning was vivid and bright, he saw a human being struggling with the elements for the last time, for while he looked the man fell forward on his face, apparently exhausted. Claude, quick as thought, caught an object in the forest to mark the line where he fell. He and Tom rushed to the place, regardless of the elements that appeared to be engaged in a war of destruction. They reached him, and found him exhausted and helpless, and apparently lifeless. Soon he was in the arms of these two stout, brave men, and was carried safely and tenderly to the place of refuge, where kind hearts would watch over him with unceasing care, until he was warmed back into life, hope, and joy.

The life of the hunter is saved, and it is hoped that the poor fleeing deer has escaped the fangs of the ruthless pursuing hounds.

The stranger was so exhausted in his efforts to reach the cottage that he was near his last hour, and far from being conscious of where he was, or what had happened. His clothing was completely saturated with the drenching rain. Claude, with the aid of Tom, soon had him laid on a soft couch with dry clothing. Then came the tender, loving charge of the good old mother, and the wife, so true, so loving, with a heart that had through years and years of service, with faithful charity for all who suffered in misfortune, for all whose sad life appealed for pity and compassion.

Soon it was evident that good nursing was restoring him to life, animation, and consciousness. With gentle slumber, and sweet repose and quiet, and the stranger passed the night, and did not awake until the morning sun with golden beams, proclaimed the glad tidings that the storm had ended, and once more there was peace on earth.

Book XIV.

PALACE VILANI.

I.

THE FLOWER-GIRL.

WHEN Phidias wrought out of the dull marble, the wonderful figure of the Olympian Jupiter, he made a fame that was imperishable. The inspiration of his exalted genius gave immortality to every touch of his supreme skill. He worked far better than he knew.

Iphi, the Greek flower girl, without ambition, without pride, had become the absolute mistress of the Vilani palace. Not by force of human genius, but by that power, born of truth and love, crowned with the never-fading laurels of victory.

She had dispelled the sombre shadows of evil that had in former years gathered around this household. She had saved a soul that was on the verge of the abyss. She had saved a human being from the ghastly death of the gibbet, and placed her in the arms of the angels of charity and mercy, who hailed her as a new born sister, and breathed into her soul the joy of an immortal life. She wrought better than she knew.

It was not like the triumph of the genius of art or of war: it was the triumph of virtue, working by the inspiration of the Infinite on a human soul on earth, dwelling in accord with his attributes of love and mercy.

THE INSANE COUNT'S RETURN. Page 215.

About the period of time that Uncle Louis had received a letter from Paul Lorraine, well on towards the close of day, the Lady Countess De Vilani and Iphi, were on the grand portico of the palace, enjoying the delightful breeze wafted from the sea. The countess was seated on a capacious arm-chair, fashioned somewhat after the seat Phidias had carved for his Grecian Jupiter. Iphi was standing leaning with an arm resting gently on the shoulder of the countess, occasionally looking out on the glad waters with golden, rippling lights, and azure shadows; again upon the happy, joyful Countess De Vilani, whom she loved so well. She had the heaven-born tenderness of a mother's love. The lost had been found. The sea of despair had thrown up upon its shining shore the priceless pearl that vice had thrown into its dark waters. Iphi's love was like the love of the good-hearted father, who killed the fatted calf for the returning prodigal, coming back to the hearth and home of his childhood years.

The faith, hope, and charity, that now glowed upon the classic features of the countess, made her charming. The base flatterers, who in her days of pride and ambition, had bowed to her the knee of heartless praise and adulation, had departed far away in the distance, and knew her not; while to the good, the true, and the virtuous, she was as a priceless jewel that had been returned to its casket.

Had Angelo carved from marble the image of Iphi, with her face so radiant with love for her dear countess, the work of art would have passed down through the coming ages as the poetic ideal of the good and the beautiful.

With joy, Iphi exclaimed, "Oh, my dear lady! I see such a beautiful ship coming into the harbor. It has such a beautiful flag on the top-gallant mast. It must be a good ship, my lady, for it sails so proudly over the waters. I will go get the large telescope, and will make out what is the name of the ship, and the country of the flag."

" Well, dear Iphi, just as you please," said the countess.

Soon Iphi returned, arranged the telescope, and fixed it upon the advancing ship.

" My lady," exclaimed Iphi. " It has thirteen stars on an azure field, on the upper corner, next the staff."

" What else is there on the flag ? " asked the countess.

" It has stripes running horizontally, alternating with red, white, and blue. And, my lady, the flag is so beautiful! The ship moves along on the waters so gracefully with its flag of shining stars. It looks like a ship of dreamland, coming out of the sky upon the joyful, dancing waters, of the sea."

" Dearest Iphi, it is the flag of the young Republic across the western sea. Each star represents a state. The red, the white, and the blue, are emblems of liberty, equality, and fraternity. The stripes, or bands, are emblems of cruel oppression. The brave sons of this land of freedom, assembled together as brothers upon the broad plan of equality and said to one another, 'We will be free. No longer shall the tyrant rule over us; we will strike until every band is riven. Our battle-cry, liberty or death.' They were victorious, and now, instead of stripes and bondage, they are free and among the constellation of nations. These states, are in truth, stars."

" Oh, my lady," exclaimed Iphi, " is that not beautiful. This then is the land of the star-spangled banner. 'The land of the free and the home of the brave.' Surely God must have been with them, when they were so weak and helpless, and struggling with the most powerful nation in the world."

" Yes, dearest Iphi, God was ever present with them and
their commander and chief, Washington. Can you tell the
name of the ship?"

" I will look, my lady, and as the ship has got much
nearer to us, I think I can find the name."

After a little time, Iphi discovered the name on a
streamer pendant from the same mast to which was fastened the flag. It read, "The Lafayette of New Orleans."

" My lady," exclaimed Iphi, "the ship is called 'The
Lafayette of New Orleans.'"

" That is so appropriate, Iphi, it is in honor of that
brave and good man who went from France to those States
with an army of Frenchmen, to assist them in their struggle for liberty."

" Then, my lady, they must love and honor Lafayette
and France, for such noble, generous aid, in the hour of
their great adversity."

" They do honor Lafayette, and such noble and brave
people are always grateful. Whenever the artists of Italy
paint a picture, or carve a statue of Washington, they
make one for Lafayette, for they were twin brothers in the
cause of American liberty."

" Oh, my lady, you have made me love that country so
much. I believe it is designed as an asylum for the oppressed of every land. How I would like to go there and
see those people, whose actions have been so glorious."

" Yes, Iphi, this Republic is grand and glorious. It has
a golden promise of greatness far beyond, and brighter
than the ancient republics of Greece and Rome. Their
government to-day, as far as a government can make
mortal man feel that he is a man, and exalt him to the
proud position of a perfect freemen is far, very far ahead

of any government that has yet appeared on earth. It has filled the whole western sky with radiant splendor. The good and the true everywhere, in every clime and country hail it as the morning star of promise to all mankind ; that the day of complete redemption from all and every kind of bondage has been inaugurated on earth."

Iphi threw her arms around the neck of the countess, exclaiming, " Oh, my lady, how I love you for these noble words. How I thank our heavenly Father that you are now so true and good, and that you have gifts of beauty, talent, and generous love, and mercy for mankind."

The countess kissed the cheek of the flower-girl, and for an instant tears of gratitude sparkled in her eyes.

" I have just thought of it, Iphi ; you recollect that Alonzo has been telling us how finely Francisco and Calvetti have been getting along, travelling all through the United States, and that he could not tell what moment they would come home and settle down in retirement, and further, that Francisco was much improved since he left Leghorn, and who knows but they may be on this very ship that has just arrived in the harbor. I will take the telescope, dear Iphi, and see if I can determine anything further about this American ship, that has been so very interesting to us both." The countess took the glass, and after examining the vessel for a little time, she said to Iphi, " She has cast anchor." The boat is lowered, and the passengers are preparing to go ashore. I see the captain of the vessel, with the dress of an American sea-captain. He is a large, commanding man in person, and looks like a brave, noble man ; fit representative of such a people as the Americans. I see a passenger descending to the boat; mercy! I believe it is Francisco Vilani, and there standing in the boat to receive him is Calvetti. Is it not strange. There is a third man whom I cannot recognize, standing beside Calvetti. You take the glass, Iphi, and see if you can make out who this stranger is, who is evidently a companion of Francisco and Calvetti."

Iphi took the glass, raised it to the proper position. "My dearest lady, I see the strange-looking man who came to our cottage to plead with me to come to the palace, and dwell with the Lady Verono, to be to her a sister and friend. Although, my lady, it is many years ago, yet I readily recognize him as the person."

"And oh, my dearest Iphi, how I do thank thee and him, that you made the promise and have kept it so well."

"And, dear lady," said Iphi, "God knows you have more than paid me, by love and affection, for any favor I may have bestowed on you."

Iphi then turned the glass on the stranger. Oh, how unspeakable was the joy in Iphi's heart, when she recognized in the stranger, her long loved, long mourned, long lost Jean. It seemed to her that God spoke and said to her, Iphi, did I not tell thee in the hours of thy deep affliction, that I would never forsake thee, and that it should ever be well with thee and thine?

Iphi's heart was so full that she could say nothing. She sank upon the seat, buried her face in her hands, and tears of joy relieved the deep emotion of her heart.

The Lady Countess was bewildered and amazed. She exclaimed, "Oh, dearest Iphi, answer me, pray tell me, my beloved, what means it?"

The Lady Countess caught the words, "It is my Jean, my dear, long-lost Jean."

Then she knew all, saw it all. She threw her arms around Iphi and said, "Iphi, has not our Father in heaven been good to us?"

II.

CAPTAIN ETHAN SMITH.

IT was the good ship Lafayette, with our friend, Captain Ethan Allen Smith. When the ship was approaching the harbor of Leghorn, Frank Harrold, whom Iphi had recognized as her long-lost Jean, was standing on the forecastle deck, talking to Captain Smith.

"Well, my dear boy, here we are back to Leghorn," said the captain, to Frank; "some changes have taken place since you and I sailed out of this harbor. The crazy count has told me all about the noble girl, Frank, you left behind you, and we have fixed up things nicely for you. By Moses, Frank, she is equal to the best Vermont girl that can be produced. I am proud of you, Frank, and I am proud of your girl, she is the genuine stuff, Frank, I will stand to you and her all my born days. You see, Frank, the count, and his man Friday, and myself, have fixed all this in our own way, my boy, and never took your advice."

"Oh, my dear friend," said Frank, "you have done so much for me, and for my brother Claude, how can I ever repay you?"

"Frank, you are at the old story; never can pay me. What pay do I want my boy? Nothing Frank, nothing. Ever since that night, Frank, you remember my boy—not

very far from here — you have taken hold of my old
weather-beaten heart right along."

"My dearest and best friend," said Frank, "I thank
you so for your kindness. I do not know — "

" Stop! stop Frank!" said the captain ; "don't say that
word again, about pay ; hold up. By Moses, Frank, you
have paid me a thousand times, by filling my old weather-
beaten heart full of love for you, my boy.

" Now, Frank, listen here ; this is the conspiracy formed
against you. Before this ship leaves this place, up in that
palace there you are to marry the best, the prettiest girl in
all Italy. By Moses, that is the long and the short of the
yarn. Frank Harrold, in connection with Pierre Lavasse
& Co., of New Orleans, will establish a Commission and
Forwarding House in Leghorn, to run in connection with
the New Orleans House. This craft will run in connection with these two houses, besides a new craft that is on
the stocks at New Orleans. She will be a spanker. Do
you know what her name will be, my boy?"

" No, my best friend," said Frank ; "surely I do not."

"Well, Frank, she is already named 'Iphi ;' do you
understand, my boy? It is all fixed, Pierre, Claude,
count, and his cashier, are all in for it, and so is
Charley."

" My dear friend, I am so thankful to you for your
ceaseless kindness to me."

"That is all right, Frank. I know all about that, you
know I do, but don't say pay any more, as if I was
selling favors as a merchant buys and sells goods. I do
not want any pay ; would not take any pay, Frank. You
see, Frank, I have no kin in this world living ; all gone.
I love my country, the sea, and my three boys ; you know,

Frank, what I mean; yes, you will marry the pretty girl, live here in Leghorn, right in the big palace, I will travel the sea, with my pet children at each end of the voyage; here I will have Frank and Iphi, over yonder I will have, — you know Frank, — Charley and Eva, Claude and wife, do you see, my boy? won't that be joyful? to have my old weather-beaten heart so full of love for my adopted children? Now and then we can take sea voyages for pleasure and amusement, and this old tar will close his days full of happiness, until he slides over the vessel into the deep, deep sea to his final rest."

"My dearest friend, your every wish shall be granted. I will be guided in all things, to render you happy."

Calvetti stepped up to Captain Smith and said, "Monsieur Captain, the count go along with me to the palace, enter Alonzo's apartment by his own way. I will go with him and prepare the way for your reception."

"Sensible to the last, my noble Calvetti; humor the count by all means. When you humor him and let him have his own way, he acts and talks as sensible as any one; all right. Calvetti, humor the count, he has more good sense than two-thirds of the people who call him insane; that he has. I have always noticed that he loves freedom of action, or in other words, he loves liberty, and I am thinking, if he had have had liberty, and social intercourse in his youth, he would have had more sense, and more genuine manhood than the men who kept him confined to brood over his misfortune."

It was well on towards night, and it was concluded that they would all go ashore, — Francisco and Calvetti, to the palace, and Captain Smith and Frank, would return on ship board, and in the morning, call on the inmates of the palace.

The plain seaman, Captain Smith, was embarrassed with the idea that he was going to pay his address to an actual countess, when he had never spoken to one.

Servants were waiting for them at the gate, and at the entrance into the grand hall, from the portico. Alonzo and the countess were ready to receive them in the drawing-room. Alonzo advanced, and extended his hand to the captain and Frank, in the most kind and cordial manner, with a heartfelt welcome.

The captain seeing that a countess was just like other very pretty women, stepped towards her and said, " Noble lady, I am Captain Ethan Smith, of the ship Lafayette."

"And my friend," said the countess; " I know you well, you are most welcome to this house. Your good ship carries that beautiful flag, the stars and stripes; ensign of the grandest nation in the world. No one can be more welcome, here in this house, than you, Captain Smith."

"Madam," said Captain Smith, "you are, perhaps, too complimentary to an humble, rough seaman. But I thank you a thousand times for the compliment you pay my dear country and her flag."

" Never mind, Captain Smith, we all know you are a good friend; Francisco, Calvetti, and Alonzo here, have told us about your kindness and generosity, and we are all as happy to see you as if it were an old acquaintance. And this young gentleman, is our dear, long-lost Jean. There is a noble, true heart in this house, that will welcome Jean with a joy that is unutterable."

The Countess De Vilani opened the large folding door to the adjoining apartment, and Iphi, dressed in the plainest, neatest manner, appeared as beautiful and sweet as the fresh-blown rose with its radiant beauty. She was the personification of nature's harmony and perfect simplicity. Every one who saw her, mentally exclaimed, " Is she not beautiful ? "

Her face was glowing with perfect joy. Jean moved towards her. Iphi saw no one in the room except this long-lost idol of her heart. She laid her hand upon his shoulder, and with a smile of love in her bright, beaming eyes, and playing upon her sweet lips, said, " It is indeed, my beloved, my long-lost, long-mourned, Jean. My best beloved, has not God been good to you and me, in the long sad years that have passed away, thus to unite us again on earth, that we may journey together to that better world, in the future."

" Dearest Iphi, God alone knows how thankful I am for the love of so true a heart as thine." And he kissed from her cheek, the tear of joy that glistened there, as the emblem of the purity of her love and her gratitude for the supreme happiness of this moment.

Captain Smith could not restrain himself, he was so much overjoyed with the appearance of Frank's pretty girl, — as he called her — that he came forward, grasped her hand, and said, " Frank is my son, you are my daughter, you are for all the world just like a very pretty American girl, you are, by Mos — yes, that is a fact, and I am going to have a kiss, Iphi, and I don't care the snap of my finger if Frank does get jealous of me."

Frank replied by saying, " My dear friend, if you only knew the fine things that Francisco and Calvetti have been telling Iphi and the countess about your kindness and generosity, to all their friends, you would see that I have more cause to be jealous than you are aware of."

" Really, my boy," said the captain, " you have talked

so much to me about Iphi, that I was in love with her before I saw her."

" Iphi, I have built a new ship, larger and better every way than the 'Lafayette.' And what name do you suppose I have given this fine ship ? "

" My dear friend, of course I cannot tell."

" I have named her 'Iphi, of Leghorn,' after the best and prettiest girl in all Italy, by Mos — yes that is her name."

" And this new ship you have built and called after me, will carry the stars and stripes ; what an honor you have paid me, our good friend."

' Yes, Iphi, she will ever carry aloft the starry banner, and never shall that flag be taken down by the hands of an American sailor at the bidding or command of an enemy. They may sink her with shot and shell, but flag and ship go down together."

" Oh, I am full of thanks to you for your kindness to our dear friends, Captain. I have in the last few hours learned all about your noble, generous actions, and I am very grateful to you."

" Never mind about that, Iphi, it is nothing. I have been paid and repaid a thousand times. Frank is a good boy, and dear to me as if my own son. Never mind about that, Iphi, I am nothing but a rough, weather-beaten sea captain."

Frank and Iphi sat down and had some talk to themselves, not intended for other ears, while the countess, Alonzo, and the captain, gathered off in one end of the apartment, and were consulting and planning the welfare and happiness of Jean and Iphi. Captain Smith seemed anxious that Frank and Iphi should be married forthwith,

as the Lafayette was to depart in a few days for other ports
in the Mediterranean, before returning to New Orleans.
So it was concluded that the wedding should take place
that very evening. They informed Frank and Iphi of their
conclusion, and the captain and Frank went out into the
city to make arrangements accordingly. That evening the
splendid apartment selected for this happy marriage was
beautifully decorated. There was present the aged parents
of Iphi, full of thankfulness that their lives had been pro-
longed to witness the marriage of their darling child to
her first love. They rejoiced that Jean was so worthy of
her, and had been so true and faithful in all things. They
had rejoiced in the good news that their favorite Louis
was doing so well.

Francisco was present with his strange, weird look, but
no one was more pleased with the happiness of these
young folks, than he. While sitting there and thinking
of Iphi, how nobly she had clung to Verono and saved
her, and that Verono was so happy and joyful, and so
much changed for good, he mentally exclaimed, "Thanks!
thanks to this noble maiden, so full of true generosity!"

Calvetti was present, and to him it was a joyful occurrence; he thought these events had worked wonders in
favor of his charge and ward, Francisco.

The priest was present, ready to perform the ceremony
at the appointed hour. Jean and Iphi, accompanied by
Captain Smith and the countess, came into the apartment,
and Jean and Iphi were thus united in marriage by the
names of Frank Harold and Iphi Vilani, as had been
agreed upon for certain reasons suggested by the good
sense of Calvetti and Captain Smith. Frank was to go
into business here in Leghorn, and it was deemed ad-
visable for him to use that name.

It was further intended that Frank and Iphi would be heirs to the greater portion of the family wealth, and then his name would be changed by law to that of Vilani.

Thus virtue has triumphed, and these two faithful hearts have been crowned with all the earthly bliss that usually fall to the lot of mankind.

The two sacks of gold, the one fastened with wire, the other with a string, were in a few days opened and used as a basis of starting the Forwarding and Commission House in Leghorn, styled, The House of Harrold, Lavasse & Co., composed of Pierre Lavasse and Charles Convors, of New Orleans, and Francis Harrold, of Leghorn, and connected with the House of Lavasse & Co., of New Orleans.

These sacks of gold had remained for so many years, that Iphi's good fortune had given her other means to help the destitute, and the unfortunate, and it now formed the basis of a commercial prosperity that blessed many a human being with happiness.

The lives of the good old parents of Iphi, closed with all the peace and harmony of a serene, cloudless sunset. There was nothing in their lives that was marked with the splendors of earth, but doubtless the portals of heaven were swung wide open to receive them, and the angels of love crowned them with wreaths of unfading splendor.

The Countess De Vilani and Iphi dwelt together with the love of sisters. Jean was faithful in the discharge of his duty, prompt, honest, and correct in all his business transactions, and of course successful.

Francisco and Calvetti spent all their time in reforming the outrageous abuses in Insane Asylums, and helping the poor.

Alonzo was not idle, he had the means, the will, and the nobleness of heart, to aid suffering humanity.

Iphi, the flower-girl, selling flowers, fruit, and vegetables in the market-place of Leghorn, to make a support for a good old father and mother who had watched over her in her infant years, and instilled in her young heart the grand principles of truth and love, had turned this palace of wealth, splendor, and crime, into an abiding place of virtue, honor, truth, and love. She found it darkened with the shadows of sin, she brought the sunlight of perfect joy. It was the triumph of faith and virtue. Her majestic soul was illumed with Promethean fire from heaven's altar, and when in years back she said, "I would sooner die than suffer dishonor," she had put on the armor of Achilles, and defied the weapons of the ruthless, merciless enemies of mankind.

This palace was the home of Iphi; she was its sunlight, its joy, its glory. She was like a column, carved with peerless elegance and beauty, standing alone in grand solitude, amidst the crumbling ruins of some ancient temple, that had long since fallen, and left this solitary mark of its departed grandeur.

ACHILLES MURAT MAKES HIMSELF KNOWN IN LOUISIANA. Page 232

BOOK XV.

THE STRANGER.

I.

" 'Tis strange, because 'tis true."

THE stranger rescued from the tempest by Claude and the negro boy Tom, arose at a late hour in the morning, refreshed and invigorated by sweet repose. He looked around the neatly furnished little bed-room, and saw from the pictures on the wall, and the fashion and form of everything, that he was in the hands of his countrymen. After he had made his toilet, Tom came into the apartment with coffee and refreshments and said, " Massa, I bring you something make you feel better, sure. "

The stranger thanked Tom for his kindness and followed his advice, and found, as Tom had said, most excellent viands for refreshment.

Claude, his mother, and wife, had assembled in the sitting-room adjoining the chamber, to receive the stranger and pay him their addresses.

When the stranger advanced into the room, Claude met him, grasped his hand and said, " Monsieur, you may think my question somewhat indiscreet, but pardon me; your face impresses me so strangely that I cannot refrain from asking your name."

" My friend," he replied, " this is the only question I cannot answer. I might give you a false name; but he who bears my name cannot lie, and I prefer to be silent; and now I cannot consistently ask the name of my benefactor who has saved my life."

"The name I bear in this country is Claude Harrold. I am not ashamed of my name in France; but there are reasons why I should be silent."

"It is the same with me," replied the stranger. "This is your mother, and this lady is your wife?"

"Yes," replied Claude.

"I will never tell my name," continued the stranger, "except to those who deserve to know it. I see you are exiles from our beloved country, France. I see further, that you are friends and will not betray me. I am Achilles Murat, son of the late king of Naples."

At the mention of this great name, they bowed their heads in love, veneration, and gratitude, and wept.

The prince being at this time a citizen of the United States, seeing this excessive emotion, evidently beyond control, was struck with great amazement. He stood silent, thinking of this strange event. He was an exile from his native country; had been out hunting for amusement; a terrible storm came upon him. He saw a light shining in the window of this humble cottage, and while struggling to reach it, fell helpless and exhausted, and his life was in peril. They heard his cry for help and saved him from death. What can all this mean?

When Claude had become calm, after the astonishment at the name of the stranger, he took him by the hand and led him to the picture we have described in a former chapter, and drawing aside a veil that covered it, he said to the prince, there is the picture of your glorious father. It was a large painting, and represented the king of Naples

on horseback, dashing along the shore of the sea, with
Vesuvius in the distance, belching forth lurid flames.
"Yes, it is your father, he is the divinity, the saint of this
household. To us all, he is next in devotion to the One
who is above all things of earth. All I have, he gave me.
I was condemned to death ; he gave me life. I was poor,
and all I have of property or goods, he gave me. And
now, if his son needs my arm, my property, my life, they
are his."

"Generous, noble man !" replied the prince ; "it is the
image of my beloved father. But in the name of heaven,
tell me! who are you that thus worship the memory of
my father? And yourself, your good old mother, and
wife, cannot refrain from tears, at the mention of his
name. Who can you be ? tell me?"

"I am Paul Lorraine. This is my dear, old mother.
This, my beloved wife, Annetta."

"Why, that cannot be! Let us be seated, and I will
tell you. My father often spoke with great tenderness of
Paul Lorraine, Jean, and Louis, who were executed at Leghorn ; also of your good mother, and your wife Annetta,
and of a Greek maiden, called Iphi, who loved Jean tenderly. I was so much interested in this event, that I examined the record of the garrison at Leghorn, and it was
recorded, that on the 19th day of June, A. D. 1808,
Paul Lorraine, Jean Gendron, and Louis Dejon, were shot
for mutiny and insubordination, with a note on the margin,
in my father's own handwriting. These young men died
heroic. They died more in honor, than dishonor. They
deserve to be honored, for they accepted death rather than
dishonor. How can it be, that you are Paul Lorraine?
Perhaps you can explain this strange mystery?"

"Dear brother! I call you dear brother, for you are as dear to me as a brother. I told you that your father had given me life when I was condemned to die. On the evening of the 18th of June, A. D. 1808, we were led into the presence of your father, then king of Naples, to receive the sentence of death. Your father could hardly restrain his sorrow for us when he was condemning us to death. He seemed to be moved with intense pity and compassion. We left his presence with no other thought than to prepare for death on the following day. We never thought of pardon, for that was impossible, as your father had, on his own responsibility, modified the absolute commands of the emperor, to put to death every man who was acting in mutiny, without even a court martial. We were marched to the place of execution, prepared to die. I noticed that the officiating sergeant did not belong to the regiment, and was unknown to me. The two men who brought the coffins on trunnels, were also strangers, and were acting as undertakers. We were placed at the head of our respective coffins, while a platoon was marched out of the regiment. We stood facing the platoon, twenty paces distant. When all was ready, the sergeant took us by the hand, and while kissing us on the cheek, quickly and distinctly said to each of us, fall at the word fire. Saved. We saw at once what it meant; that your father had planned to save our lives; keep the good will of the emperor, and set an example to the army, that such breaches of discipline had to be punished with death.

We fell at the fire of the platoon. The two strangers came forward, and, with the assistance of the sergeant, we were placed in the coffins. The platoon was marched into the regiment, and the regiment marched back into the garrison. Being on the outside of the Pisan gate, we were not far from the cemetery. By some kind of contrivance, the lids of the coffins were fastened, yet we could with some difficulty breathe. By this time it was quite dark. When we reached the cemetery gate, there was some conversation which I could not hear distinctly, but we moved on again, and soon were at the place where three graves had been dug to receive us.

We were hastily taken out of the coffins, and our dress as soldiers of France was taken off, and we each put on the blue uniform of American seamen, while our French uniforms were put in the coffins and buried in the graves.

The sergeant gave us each a package containing one thousand francs, with an order to the officers in charge of the ship, Lafayette, laying in the harbor, to receive us as employees. This order was signed by Captain Ethan Smith. We also had a pass from the king of Naples, with instructions to destroy it when safe on board of ship.

We could not read these orders, for it was quite dark, but were informed of their contents. Then we were led to a back passage of the cemetery, with directions what course to take to reach the vessel in the harbor.

When on board the ship, we recognized Captain Smith and the mate, as the persons who had assisted in the execution and burial of the empty coffins.

When we were out on the sea, and under way with full sail, you can form no idea, my dear Prince, of the love and gratitude that Louis, Jean, and myself, felt towards your father for thus preserving our lives.

It was very sad and distressing for me to leave my mother, and my wife, and my dear native land; for Jean to leave Iphi, whom he loved so well; and Louis his dear parents. But we were young and full of hope; and thanks to our heavenly Father that our hopes have been realized.

Captain Smith informed us that on the morning of the day of the execution, your father sent for him, desiring very strongly for him not to fail, as he wanted to see him on pressing business. When together it was planned that one of the king's faithful attendants should attend to the execution, as a sergeant of his body guard. Captain Smith was to bring an assistant, and to come with coffins as undertakers, with the dress of an American seaman in each coffin, to be exchanged in the cemetery.

Captain Smith, in relating this interview, said that when your father told him what kind of boys we were, he said to your father, " By Moses, he would see the boys' through; take 'em to New Orleans and set them up."

The prince heard this strange recital with astonishment, and saw in it a new development of the noble-hearted character of his father. " He performed this act of mercy, to gratify the goodness of his heart, and thus conceal it from the world. Is it not very strange that I should have been in a storm, my life in peril, and you, of all the men on this earth, should come to me and save me from death ?"

Annetta, in her sweet, plaintive tone of voice, said to him, " Dear Prince, it is not strange ; you were sent to us so that we could express to the son our love and gratitude for the father who saved the life of our dear Paul. God said to Paul, there is one dying in the tempest, whom you love with a brother's love, and you would give everything to save him from death. Put a light in the window to lead him to this house of refuge, under the protection of a love that will endure beyond the grave. God surely has done this all for us." The voice and manner of Annetta was so full of pathos that tears stood in the eyes of the prince as he listened to the sincere and earnest avowal, that God had directed him to this humble cot for protection.

The prince now inquired of Paul, where this Captain Smith was at the present time. Paul informed him that he was still engaged in the shipping business, between the ports of the Mediterranean and New Orleans; and the last time he saw him in New Orleans he informed him that he expected to die on the sea. That the ship on the ocean had been his cradle, and the waves should be his winding-sheet and grave. During the late war with England he had command of a war vessel, and was a terror upon the sea. " He is brave, generous, and noble-hearted. He had, after all danger of compromising your father was passed, made arrangement to bring my mother, wife, Uncle Louis, and his two sons from Marseilles to New Orleans; arrangements having been previously made for them to be at Marsailles on a certain day, to meet him there with his ship ' Lafayette.'

" Uncle Louis and his two sons are in New Orleans, and doing well. Louis Dejon is there, a successful merchant, under the name of Charles Convors; he became the partner of Pierre Lavasse, and the husband of his daughter. Jean Gendron, under the name of Frank Harrold, went back years ago, and married Iphi; went into business in connection with Louis at New Orleans, and has been very prosperous and happy. Captain Smith has ever been a good friend to us all, and every time I think of him, and what he has done for Louis, Jean, and myself, my heart is filled with gratitude and love for him. And now we would all like to hear of the last days of your father."

The prince in reply, said his father had been "betrayed by his pretended friends, into the hands of his enemies. And on the 13th day of October, 1815, he was put to death by the order of Ferdinand. The 13th of October has been a day of mourning for us all, as each year brings around its sad memories. He was kind and generous to every one. When he heard that Paris had surrendered, and the emperor was a prisoner in the hands of his enemies, he wept tears of sorrow, and said to my mother, 'Caroline,' all is lost.' 'No,' said my mother, in that lofty, imperial spirit of her brother. 'No, all is not lost. We have preserved honor, and constancy remains to us in adversity.' He listened with composure to his sentence of death, and sat down and wrote these words, — I have a copy of this letter, but every word is engraven on my heart and memory : —

"'DEAR CAROLINE.— My last hour is sounded. In a few moments I shall have ceased to live, and you will no longer have a husband. Do not forget me. My life has been stained by no injustice. Farewell, my Letitia ; farewell, my Achilles ; farewell, my Lucian ; farewell, my Louisa. I leave you without fortune or kingdom, in the midst of enemies. Be united and prove yourselves superior to misfortune. Remember that my greatest suffering is dying far from my children. Receive my blessing, my embrace, and my tears. Preserve, ever in your memory, the recollection of your unhappy father. JOACHIM.'

"My beloved father asks us to remember him. How dear his memory has been to us all! He is ever present with us in memory. Each year, as the 13th day of October comes around, I spend the day in silence and tears.

" He said, in the last hour of his life, that it was to him a sweet consolation, that he never saw the face of a man who fell by his hand ; for if he had, his image would have rendered his life miserable. He was brave, kind-hearted, just, and merciful. Yet, in the hour of his cruel death, there was no one to pity him, no one to show him pardon and mercy."

The prince could no longer control his emotions, and was silent for some time, when good Mother Lorraine said to him, " Mourn not, my son. For he had the mercy and compassion of one who was able to save, far above all kings of earth. He died in peace. He had ever been just, loving, and merciful. Fear not, my son ; God never has, nor ever will forsake such a one as he. When this good soul left earth, the outstretched arms of the great Shepherd led him through the shadows of death, to the kingdom of the blest."

" Good mother, I do believe he is in heaven, for he was good and just. When he stood before his enemies to die, he said, ' Do not darken my eyes.' He smiled on the weapons of death, and said, ' Fire at my heart ! ' and clasped to his bosom the image of his wife and children.

" His eyes were fixed upon the clear, serene Italian sky, and doubtless, far away in the azure depths, he saw the shining throne, and hope heard the sweet songs of the angels of charity and mercy."

The last words of the prince were uttered in broken sobs. They all bowed their heads and wept in silence. The prince and the peasant wept together.

If ever the immortal soul that has passed the barriers of earth comes back to receive the sweet and holy incense of love, gratitude, and adoration, offered on the altar by unselfish hearts, the majestic soul of Joachim Murat was present with them in this humble cottage home.

The sun had arisen high up in the sky with golden beams, proclaiming peace and joy once more to the storm-beaten earth. The passing wind sighed mournfully over the ruin and wreck of field and forest.

The prince and the peasant lived and loved as brothers. Negro Tom, who had ever been faithful, was emancipated, as he was the first to hear the cry for help. Paul Lorraine said to him, "Never more shall man call thee slave."

Years have passed away. Not far from this cottage, on the roadside leading to New Orleans, in a cemetery there are three graves, side by side. They are covered with marble slabs. On one is carved the name of Annetta. One is the grave of the peasant soldier, who pointed the pathway to the greatest commander of modern times in his triumphant march across the Alps, in the cause of justice and liberty. The other is the grave of the good mother, whose sublime faith ever said to her heart, in the end all will be well. They rest beneath the cloud, rainbow, sun, and stars. The shadow of the cyprus, pine, magnolia, and the vine, redolent with the incense of blossoms and flowers, falls gently and lovingly upon their last resting-place.

Three grand souls passed this way from earth to heaven. Their lives had been poor and humble, without pride, without ostentation, but embellished with the splendid virtues of love, charity, and mercy.

THE END.

www.ingramcontent.com/pod-product-compliance
Lightning Source LLC
Chambersburg PA
CBHW030407270326
41926CB00009B/1316